RECEIVED OCT 2018 BY:

NO LONGER PROPERTY OF SEATTLE PUBLIC LIBRARY

"I so desire to belong to a beloved community where I and all are welcome, and we are called to fully explore our pathways to spiritual health, healing, and wholeness. *True Inclusion* provides us all with resources necessary to build such a community. This book will be a vital tool for those who feel called to recreate the Body of Christ in the image and likeness of a God who, as Peter preached in Acts 10, shows no partiality." —John C. Dorhauer, General Minister and President, The United Church of Christ

"More and more congregations across the country are fully welcoming LGBTQ+ people into their communities as leaders, pastors, and members. It's high time. But creating a culture of genuine inclusion takes skill and intentionality. Brandon knows this firsthand as a young gay man raised in an evangelical tradition. In *True Inclusion*, Brandon shares his story and in doing so gives congregations a roadmap for talking about our hopes and fears, our theological questions, and our lived experiences as we wrestle with widening the welcome of the Body of Christ. If your church is committed to a wide welcome and radical inclusion of all of God's children, this is a great resource for you." —Cameron Trimble, CEO, Center for Progressive Renewal and Convergence Network

"In *True Inclusion*, Brandan Robertson presses us to move beyond the performative—to truly follow a Christ who gave up godly power in order to stand in solidari Brandan lays out clearly why the inclusion e for the church today, and offers tions for every Christian community to pastors who want to avoid allyship o pursues justice and equality for people ntations." —Austen Hartke, author of *Transforming: The Bible and the Lives of Transgender Christians*

"Brandan has done such a fantastic job helping us to think better about taking off the blinders that we use to exclude people who aren't like us, and to look deeper into understanding those whose experience we may not fully understand. In his new book *True Inclusion* he challenges us to better understand the privileges we so often can take for granted, and to step outside of our comfort zones to not only embrace the ones on the margins but to live out there." —Trey Pearson, singer, songwriter

"Brandan is a crucial and courageous theologian working at the intersection between faith and LGBTQ equality. In *True Inclusion* he delivers a strong, but much needed, challenge to all churches. He asks pastors and congregations to reassess how welcoming they truly are to LGBTQ people and other diverse demographics. Brandan calls out lukewarm attempts and fearful silence, asking instead for bold commitment. *True Inclusion* is an excellent handbook to help churches on their journey toward mirroring God's radically inclusive love."
—Vicky Beeching, speaker, LGBTQ equality campaigner, and author of *Undivided: Coming Out, Becoming Whole and Living Free From Shame*

"Don't read this book unless you want to be challenged: challenged to love, love yourself, God, and neighbor; challenged to include, to truly include; challenged to love as Christ loves us; challenged to walk the gospel road of inclusion. *True Inclusion* is written with a style and a viewpoint that is grounded in evangelical Christianity yet will challenge us all to continue our journey, working to build the Kingdom of God 'where there is unity in the midst of great diversity, where we are not forced to abandon the multiplicity of identities that make us unique, but where the gifts that those identities produce are embraced and celebrated.'" —Mark Johnston, executive director, The Disciples LGBTQ Alliance

"Despite greater conversations and movement toward equality in the church, we still have an incredible amount of work before us to create communities that truly embody full inclusion for all. Brandan Robertson's prophetic and wise voice is a much-needed gift to the Body of Christ during these changing times! He anchors us in a deep Jesus-centered theology and challenges us to courageous leadership and practice that will transform not only our own lives and churches but also the wider world. *True Inclusion* stirs, challenges, and inspires."
—Kathy Escobar, copastor of The Refuge and author *of Faith Shift: Finding Your Way Forward When Everything You Believe is Coming Apart*

TRUE
INCLUSION

CREATING COMMUNITIES
OF RADICAL EMBRACE

BRANDAN ROBERTSON

chalice
press

Saint Louis, Missouri

An imprint of Christian Board of Publication

Copyright ©2018 by Brandan Robertson

All rights reserved. For permission to reuse content, please contact Copyright Clearance Center, 222 Rosewood Drive, Danvers, MA 01923, (978) 750-8400, www.copyright.com.

All scripture quotes, unless otherwise indicated, are the author's paraphrase.

Scripture quotations marked (NIV) are taken from the HOLY BIBLE, NEW INTERNATIONAL VERSION®. NIV®. Copyright © 1973, 1978, 1984 by International Bible Society. Used by permission of Zondervan Publishing House. All rights reserved.

Scripture quotations marked (CEV) are taken from the *Contemporary English Version.* Copyright © 1991, 1992, 1995 by American Bible Society. Used by Permission.

Scripture taken from The Voice™. Copyright © 2008 by Ecclesia Bible Society. Used by permission. All rights reserved.

Scripture marked NASB is taken from the *NEW AMERICAN STANDARD BIBLE®,* © Copyright The Lockman Foundation 1960, 1962, 1963, 1968, 1971, 1972, 1973, 1975, 1977. Used by permission.

Cover design: Vicky Vaughn Shea of Ponderosa Pine Design. Copyright ©2018. All rights reserved.

Cover art: ©iStockphoto

ChalicePress.com

Print: 9780827237186
EPUB: 9780827237193
EPDF: 9780827237209

Printed in the United States of America

To LaSalle Street Church in Chicago,
for being the first community to embody true inclusion for me,
when I wasn't yet able to include myself

Contents

Acknowledgments   viii

Introduction   1

1. Explaining Exclusion   5

2. Missing the Mark   16

3. The Inclusion Imperative   27

4. The Importance of Inclusion   39

5. The Problem of Patriarchy   53

6. The Ingredients of Inclusion   67

7. Inclusion in Context   82

Conclusion   103

Appendices:
1. Making True Inclusion Real in Your Context:
     10 Suggested Actions   109

2. Resources for Further Study   117

Acknowledgments

This book was one that both flowed seamlessly and was incredibly challenging to write. The concepts of intersectional inclusivity have been embedded in my understanding of the Christian faith for as long as I can remember. Nonetheless, some of the insights and ideas that I share in this book have challenged me and shaken up my faith in crucial ways. I hope that they do the same for you.

Also, as any author will tell you, a book is never the product of a single person, but a single person channeling the ideas, love, and support of a multitude. Because of this, there are always many people to thank when a book is birthed into the world.

First, I want to thank Deborah Arca for sitting down with me on that sunny afternoon at Union Station in Denver and pitching the idea for this book. I didn't know how much *I* needed to write this book then, and I have greatly appreciated your encouragement and insight throughout this process.

To the entire team at Chalice Press: thank you for helping me to create this book and for believing in its message. I am deeply grateful.

To the church I have the honor of pastoring, Missiongathering Christian Church in San Diego: thank you for helping me to think through the concepts in this book and experiment with them on you (even when you didn't know you were being experimented on!). The Spirit of inclusion is at your heart, and I am so honored to be able to step into the work that God has already begun in your midst and continue to journey forward with you all.

To my friends, teachers, and mentors who have shaped and challenged my idea of what it means to be truly inclusive: Dr. Floyd Thompkins, Dr. David Anderson, Dr. Sharon Groves, Fr. Richard Rohr, Rob Bell, Dr. Miguel De La Torre, Dr. Jennifer Leath, Dr. J.R. Daniel Kirk, Dr. Brian McLaren, Dr. Diana Butler Bass, Teresa Pasquale, Bishop Paul Colton, Bishop Gene Robinson, Bishop Karen Oliveto, Bishop Joseph Tolton, Matthew Vines, Vicky Beeching, Jayne Ozanne, and many more. Your collective wisdom and insight has shaped and molded me in too many ways to recount. Thank you for your work and witness.

To my friends, for putting up with my endless ramblings about this book as I wrote it and for supporting me in this season of my own journey: Isaac, Andy, Jacob, Quinton, Rich, Lee, Rebekah, Cameron, Troy, Jeremiah, and Michael.

And to you, the reader: thank you for picking up this book and exploring the concepts and practices of inclusion. I believe that places like this are starting points, and I hope and pray you continue to lean into this radically subversive gospel of inclusion, and that your life and world are transformed by it.

"He drew a circle that shut me out—

Heretic, rebel, a thing to flout.

But love and I had the wit to win:

We drew a circle and took him in."

—Edwin Markham, "Outwitted"

Introduction

"It's just our hope that you don't leave here and start waving rainbow flags."

The dean of students at my Bible college spoke these words to me at the beginning of my senior year. I had been called into a meeting with the dean and my choir director on the first day of classes after another professor had circulated among the entire faculty photos of me with some well-known LGBT+ clergy at a festival that summer. There was "concern," they said, about the company I was keeping and whether it reflected my personal theology.

You see, for a majority of Christians around the world, to be inclusive and embracing of LGBT+ people is to abandon true Christianity. This is certainly still the case in the conservative evangelical movement of which my Bible college was a part, churning out thousands of students every year to lead the Church in the fight against the culture, which is growing more and more accepting of the "unacceptable"—namely, the lives and relationships of sexual and gender minorities.

Beyond the exclusively evangelical and fundamentalist denominational spheres, there are many more denominations that have chosen to call themselves "welcoming" to LGBT+ people, but that still retain a homophobic undercurrent that prevents LGBT+ individuals from becoming truly *embraced* for the fullness of our gifts and perspectives. And, of course, there are also those denominations that have been in the vanguard of the fight for full inclusion of sexual and gender minorities, led by brave saints like my friend Bishop Gene Robinson, who fully welcome and celebrate LGBT+ people at every level of church leadership. These denominations march in their local pride parades, proudly hang rainbow flags in front of their churches, and use gender inclusive language in all of their hymns and scripture readings. They're truly and deeply inclusive.

But is all of that *really* enough?

• • •

1

This book is an accessible guide for individuals and faith communities who desire to embrace what I call "true inclusion." True inclusion calls us beyond mere welcome, beyond outward signs of celebration, and even beyond the LGBT+ conversation itself and to a completely new paradigm for how we live our faith in the confines of our sanctuary and in the public square. What I propose in these pages is nothing short of a fundamental shift in posture and practice that calls communities to mirror the very posture of Jesus Christ, of whom it is written that he, *"being God in his nature, did not consider his equality with God something to be exploited, so he humbled himself, taking on the form of a servant... Therefore, God exalted him"* (Phil. 2:5-8).[1]

As those who claim to follow in the rhythms of Jesus, we must to learn to do exactly what Christ did himself. This begins by recognizing who we are; identifying our privilege; and willingly giving up our positions of privilege for the good of the silenced, marginalized, and oppressed—and, in so doing, maximize the light and power of the Divine in and through us and our communities.

As soon as we begin this journey of self-humbling, every part of our own identity, worldview, and life becomes vulnerable to reformation. The way we believe, the way we practice, the way we worship—everything changes. True inclusion, which I believe is the very heartbeat of the Scriptures and central message of the gospel, will cause us to break down every boundary that we think is essential and throw us out into the choppy waters of *real life,* where nothing is simple, nothing is easy, but *everything is beautiful.*

This is a book for people and communities at every stage of the journey. No matter whether you're a "conservative" community that is just beginning to have conversations about the "issue" of LGBT+ inclusion, or you're a church that is fully affirming of LGBT+ people but desires to go deeper than affirmation to full embrace, each section is intended to challenge you.

The lessons, stories, and wisdom contained in these pages come from the work that I have been privileged to do since 2013, work that has permitted me to travel across North America and Europe to meet some of the most remarkable LGBT+ leaders, theologians, activists, and other individuals. They have opened their hearts and shared their experiences with me so that I might

---

1   Unless otherwise noted, scripture quotes are my paraphrase.

help other individuals and communities to begin this important journey towards true inclusion.

Back to that meeting with the dean of my Bible college: I walked out of his office that day feeling utterly afraid, shamed, and threatened with expulsion over my inclusive stance and beliefs. He had insisted that if I continued such behavior after I graduated, the "defenders of orthodoxy" would publicly question my integrity. At the time, I didn't know what to believe, I didn't know who I was, I didn't know how to identify. I was confused and afraid, a young Christian who desired only one thing: to serve God by being a pastor. Suddenly, all of my hopes and callings seemed to be hanging by a thread that depended on how well I played by the rules that I was being told God had set.

The trauma and pain that I experienced in this setting was unimaginable. And within weeks of this meeting, I was forcefully "encouraged" to begin a conversion therapy program to heal me from my "same-sex desires." All of this was to ensure that I stayed on the "right" side of the theological, social, and political aisle, instead of teetering on the edge of eternal hell—or, worse, being thrown out of the evangelical movement.

During this season, I found a small church just a few blocks from my school that identified as deeply Christian, but also deeply inclusive. Not only did this church welcome me as a closeted LGBT+ person and encourage me to take my time on my journey of self-discovery and reconciliation of my faith and sexuality, it also challenged me to take the message of the gospel to its furthest conclusion. That meant beginning to think about how to be a person that didn't merely "welcome" individuals from all genders, sexualities, ethnicities, cultures, socioeconomic statuses, disabilities, backgrounds, and religions, but also *embraced* them with God's unconditional, never-ending, all-expansive love.

Since Bible college, I've experienced the full force of Christian exclusion in many ways. In 2014, various Southern Baptist leaders took to national publications like *TIME Magazine* to condemn me and my fight for inclusion as fundamentally unchristian. I've been shamed on stage by theologians and been condescended to by Christian radio show hosts. I have also heard thousands of stories from LGBT+ people of having experienced more harm than I could ever fathom. That harm has come not only from conservative communities who exclude people outwardly, but also from within communities whose members *think* they're inclusive simply because they have a sign on the church or a rainbow flag in the sanctuary.

Since finding that small church in Chicago that challenged me and spoke words of healing and life to my fear-filled spirit, I have been committed and passionate about helping the Church reject the false gospel that excludes, and instead tap into the message of radical inclusion at the heart of the biblical narrative and Christian tradition. For me, this has taken many forms: organizing conferences that feature exclusively LGBT+ Christian speakers so that church leaders can hear our real stories and see the real impact of toxic exclusive theology; hosting closed-door meetings in Nashville, Salt Lake City, and London with the leaders and influencers of some of the largest denominations in the world; and working with political leaders in the White House and on Capitol Hill to secure full rights—not just for LGBT+ individuals, but for *all people,* without exception.

Inclusion has become a passion of mine because I deeply believe that it is the heart of God and the fundamental direction of the universe. And I believe that we are living on the brink of a new era of reformation and evolution that is causing people in every one of our social institutions to re-examine who they are and how they live as people, and to shift to be even more deeply inclusive and embracing of the complexity and diversity of humanity. True inclusion is about far more that LGBT+ inclusion, though the conversation around sexuality and gender is usually the starting point for these exchanges. Instead, inclusion is a fundamental shift in our way of seeing and being in the world that changes how we think about everything and everyone.

I hope that this book is a starting point, a launching pad, or fuel injection for your journey toward true inclusion and full embrace. This is not a perfect or comprehensive text by any means. It's simply meant to be a resource to help each of us think through how we might reform our lives to be increasingly inclusive, how we might embrace the full breadth of diversity represented in every single person.

Let's begin our journey together.

Explaining Exclusion

We've all been excluded from something before. Upon realizing that we were not invited to an event with the rest of our friends, or being told quite blatantly that we are not welcome to participate in some group or activity, we are overcome with a deep sense of shame: shame that we are not good enough; shame that we must have done something wrong to merit this exclusion—or, worse, that we must *be* something wrong. We question who we are, our place in our friend group or community, and sometimes even our fundamental self-worth. To be deliberately excluded is one of the deepest pains a human can experience, because we are fundamentally wired for community. That is how we begin to develop an individual sense of self, and how we craft the worldview and narrative by which we will live our lives.

Belonging is one of the most fundamental needs of human beings. Leading psychological researcher Brené Brown is right: "A deep sense of love and belonging is an irreducible need of all people. We are biologically, cognitively, physically, and spiritually wired to love, to be loved, and to belong. When those needs are not met, we don't function as we were meant to. We break. We fall apart. We numb. We ache. We hurt others. We get sick."[1]

According to Christian theology, our need to belong is a direct reflection of the God in whose image we're made. In orthodox Christian teaching, God is understood to be a trinity: three persons, one substance, in eternal relationship with one another. Creator, Christ, and Spirit (or Father, Son, and Holy Ghost, in

---

1   Quotation from Brené Brown found in Monika Carless and Lieselle Davidson, "The Power of Vulnerability," *Elephant Journal*, 27 Feb., 2017, www.elephantjournal.com/2017/02/power-vulnerability-brene-browns-ted-talk-may-be-the-breakthrough-youve-been-looking-for/.

more traditional language) exist as the three faces of God, three individuated parts of the same whole.

It is from these fundamental relationships at the heart of God that *Love* is generated, and, from *Love*, all of creation bursts forth. If God is fundamentally an interconnected, triune relationship, then it follows that those made in the image and likeness of God are also fundamentally wired for such relationships. As the renowned Franciscan writer Fr. Richard Rohr notes: "Everything exists in radical relationship, which we now call ecosystems, orbits, cycles, and circulatory systems... God is relationship itself... The Way of Jesus is an invitation to a Trinitarian way of living, loving, and relating—on earth as it is in the Godhead. We are intrinsically like the Trinity, living in an absolute relatedness."[2]

If belonging is truly an "irreducible need of all people" and "we are intrinsically like the Trinity, living in absolute relatedness," then exclusion and rejection from our communities of belonging is a fundamental assault on the humanity of a person. It is an assault on the fundamental order of creation, an attack on something generated from the very essence of who God is. From the Christian perspective, to exclude another person from relationship, and especially relationship to God, is perhaps the most blasphemous and destructive sin we could commit. To isolate another human being is to cut them off from the relationships that are so fundamental to what it means to be a human, and degrades the very essence of their humanity.

Furthermore, when we exclude a person or group of people, we are degrading our *own* humanity, acting not in the spirit of Christ, and not even acting like good humans. By perpetuating dehumanization, we dehumanize ourselves. Think about it: the more exclusive a community becomes, the more immorality tends to increase in those communities. Think of the most exclusive cults or secret societies in our world, and almost every single one of them has been plagued by abuse and immorality. Why? Because, whenever we exclude, we are pushing others away from their fundamental nature, and we are also degrading our own nature as humans.

---

2   Richard Rohr, *God Is Relationship*, Center for Action and Contemplation, Sept. 7, 2016, cac.org/god-is-relationship-2016-09-16/.

Isn't it ironic, then, that those who have been commissioned with the "gospel of inclusion" have, more often than not, become people of the most exclusive communities and theologies? Throughout our two-thousand-year history, Christians time and time again have fallen into the trap of dualistic thinking, declaring who is in and who is out, who is saved and who is damned, who can join communities and who is to be expelled. These behaviors have absolutely no place in the Christian narrative. Yet ask almost any passerby and they will confirm that we Christians are known more often for our exclusion than for our radical embrace of all.

Why We Exclude

Exclusion is clearly incompatible with the gospel of Christ. And yet all of us will exclude and be excluded in some way over the course of our lives. On one hand, exclusion is important to maintaining a unique identity within a family or community. We'll explore this a bit more later. When we exclude in this way, it is to preserve a unique culture or identity. This type of exclusion is not meant to marginalize others, but rather to preserve distinct values or practices of a community. The exclusion that we're focusing on is instead exclusion based on fear of difference and the human impulse to find a scapegoat for our problems.

French anthropologist René Girard has written extensively about the "scapegoating mechanism" that nearly every religion and culture throughout history adopts as a means of creating cohesion within a community.[3] By identifying an enemy that they can blame for their collective problems, whether a single person or a group of people, entire nations can be unified. Just think of moments in your lifetime when you experienced such unity. For example, on September 11, 2001, the United States—and, indeed, the Western world—experienced a unity that has rarely been reproduced. But this unity, rooted in fear, was grounded in a hatred of Islam and Muslims, who were seen not just as the perpetrators of the terrorist attacks in New York and Washington, D.C., but very quickly as the cause of all of our

---

3   Rene Girard, *The Scapegoat* (Baltimore: Johns Hopkins University Press, 1996).

problems—economic, social, and spiritual. By identifying a group of persons whom we believe to be dangerous and to pose a threat to our collective wellbeing, we create a cohesive unity driven by a desire to exclude and often destroy those we regard as the cause of our problems.

In Scripture, this scapegoating mechanism is seen clearly from the Hebrew Bible through the New Testament in the distinction between "clean" and "unclean." In the Hebrew mind, the Jewish people were the chosen and "pure" race of people, set apart by God to be the rightful rulers and brokers of justice for the world. Everyone outside of this ethnic, cultural, and religious group were regarded as "unclean" and as posing a threat to the cause of the Hebrew people. It was this exclusion and marginalization of all other cultures, races, and religions that unified the Hebrew people and enabled them to commit acts of mass murder as they fought to obtain lands that they believed were given to them by God, but were occupied by allegedly "unclean" peoples. For a Jewish person to mingle even socially with a Gentile was to become defiled, and caused at the very least a temporary exclusion from the life of the community.

This distinction between "clean" and "unclean" is carried throughout the New Testament and is seen most clearly in chapter 10 of the book of Acts. In this chapter, the apostle Peter falls into a trance, and is told by God to *"rise up, kill, and eat"* (v. 13b) unkosher (unclean) animals that were forbidden by the purity codes of the Hebrew Bible. Peter, being a faithful Jew, argues with God, claiming that he has always been faithful about remaining pure and separate from all unclean beings. It seems that he believed that God was testing him. But then the Scriptures say that God uttered revolutionary and infamous words to Peter: *"Do not call unclean that which I have made clean"* (v. 15b). In this singular phrase, we see one of the key ethical movements of the New Testament, a movement away from the distinction of "clean" and "unclean" and toward an ethic of radical inclusion. In this moment, the Spirit of God is tearing down the artificial barriers that had been created to separate humanity into divided factions, and, instead, was working to create what the apostle Paul calls "one new humanity" (Eph. 2:15, NIV).

Theologian and ethicist Miroslav Volf writes about this distinction between "clean" and "unclean" in his groundbreaking and award-winning book *Exclusion and Embrace*. It is something he knows about personally, as a Croatian public theologian: "Sin is...the kind of purity that wants the world cleansed of the other rather than the heart cleansed of the evil that drives people out by calling those who are clean 'unclean.'"[4] In Volf's analysis, the distinctions between clean and unclean, the included and the excluded, are matters of the heart, not a literal state of reality. We divide, marginalize, and exclude based on an inner "evil," which I think is simply fear. The solution to this inner fear is never to drive out the "unclean" person, but rather to rid ourselves of the "uncleanness" of our own hearts. We exclude only because of our own fear and desire for self-preservation, rooted in ignorance of the "other." It is this same fear that drove the Hebrew people (and most other cultures, both ancient and modern) to declare the people in other nations and cultures "unclean," and to create fantastic mythologies about the wicked practices of these other cultures. In this collective exclusivity and superiority, a strong, cohesive bond is formed. But that bond perpetuates a system of fear that brings destruction to everyone.

This is why God's words in Acts are so crucial: *there is nothing unclean*. And the New Testament echoes the dissolution of all false boundaries and borders with its declaration that "there is no Jew or Gentile, slave or free, male or female, for all are one!" (Gal. 3:28). The gospel calls us to abandon our fear-based versions of unity through exclusion, and embrace the way of Christ. That way calls us into proximity with our "others" through acts of radical hospitality and service, for Jesus knew that it's hard to demonize from up close. When we serve our "other," we quickly recognize our shared humanity, and we are drawn to a radical inclusivity rooted in love. As Volf concludes: "By embracing the 'outcast,' Jesus underscored the 'sinfulness' of the persons and systems that cast them out."[5]

We exclude because we are afraid, and fear is a powerful tool for unification. But the unity that emerges in exclusive systems

---

4   Miroslav Volf, *Exclusion and Embrace: A Theological Exploration of Identity, Otherness, and Reconciliation* (Nashville: Abingdon Press, 1996), 74.
5   Ibid., 72.

is a shallow, temporal unity that only harms everyone involved. The inclusive unity embodied and taught by Jesus is a unity that comes, not through recognizing our differences, but via our common humanity. At our core, we are all one. Christ is in all of us, and we all live, move, and have our being in God. In the recognition that beyond all of our identities and uniqueness we share the same common core of being, we find the key to lasting unity.

All of our divisions are human constructions with no grounding in reality. Our color, class, culture, sexuality, gender, political positions, or religious beliefs do not actually cause substantial divisions, because at the end of the day we are still human beings, participating in the same life and light. At our deepest level, we are one. But sin obscures this. Our egos create masks and draw lines where there is no need to do so. This is what Jesus came to dismantle. Whereas the rest of the world is inclined to create unity through separateness, Jesus proclaims a much more difficult but also much more generative path: unity through inclusivity. Whereas exclusion breeds only harm, inclusion leads to abundant life.

The Harm of Exclusion

In recent history, no community has experienced such fierce exclusion from Christian communities more than has the LGBT+ community. I myself have been threatened with expulsion, forced into "reparative therapy," and declared a heretic simply because I believe that God does not condemn me for my same-sex relationship and attractions. And in this modern era, there are studies on the tangible impact of exclusion on the lives of LGBT+ people who grow up in exclusive religion environments, studies that show the lasting damage that is done when faith communities, families, and individuals push sexual and gender minorities away because of what I believe are their God-given identities.

The following brief summary of some of the best of these studies comes from my book *Our Witness: The Stories of LGBT+ Christians*, in which I briefly summarize the negative impact of nonaffirming theology on the psyche of LGBT+ people:

In 2012, the European Symposium of Suicide and Suicidal Behavior released a groundbreaking survey that suggested that suicide rates among LGBT+ youth were significantly higher if the youth grew up in a religious context. Similarly, dozens of studies from 2001–2015 have found links between religious affiliation and higher rates of depression and suicidality among LGBT+ adults. A study published in 2014 by Jeremy Gibbs concluded: "[Sexual Minority Youth] who mature in religious contexts, which facilitate identity conflict, are at higher odds for suicidal thoughts and suicide attempt compared to other SMY."

Every year, new studies come out that suggest that non-inclusive religious teachings result in higher rates of depression and suicidal ideation among LGBT+ youth and adults alike. These facts must be heeded by those in Christian leadership and cause deep reflection on how their teaching and practices are complicit in these concerning trends.[6]

These numbers should concern every person who reads them, especially Christian leaders. While in the past we might have been able to get away with saying "Sticks and stones may break my bones, but words will never hurt me," the overwhelming evidence from psychological research shows that exactly the opposite is true. When we preach messages of exclusion based on fundamental and unchangeable traits and characteristics of human beings, we are doing tremendous harm that affects individuals for a lifetime.

And, of course, the effects are exacerbated when the individual being excluded is a child or young person, in the early stages of their development. Just imagine being told as a child—by leaders who are supposed to speak on behalf of God—that you are fundamentally flawed, broken, and must change yourself or else be expelled from your community and potentially even be damned to hell for eternity. The trauma and harm done to that young soul cannot be overemphasized.

---

6   Robertson, Brandan, ed., *Our Witness: The Unheard Stories of LGBT Christians* , (Eugene, Oreg.: Wipf and Stock, 2018): 2–3.

Of course, exclusion doesn't only impact the LGBT+ community. In fact, dozens of studies have been done that show that exclusion has similar effects on *everyone* who is forced from their community or social group. A National Institutes of Health study on social exclusion concluded, "Social exclusion led to a decrease in positive mood ratings and increased anger ratings."[7] A University of California, Los Angeles, study found that social exclusion literally results in physical harm to the body, including intense physical pain.[8] A similar study done by researchers in the United Kingdom concluded that social exclusion "causes a number of dysfunctional reactions including lowered self-esteem, greater anger, inability to reason well, depression and anxiety, and self-defeating perceptions and behaviours."[9] Study after study shows that exclusion from social groups has measurable negative impacts on human beings of all backgrounds.

Jesus entrusted us with a gospel that is supposed to bring life, hope, and redemption to everyone. Yet for a majority of our history, we in the Church have proclaimed a message of exclusion, death, and hopelessness to most people. Jesus himself taught that if our lives and teachings bear bad fruit, they should be disregarded as not from God (Mt. 7:19). James tells us that there is no "favoritism" with God (James 2:9). In other words, everyone who has been created is declared "very good" and stands equal in the sight of their Creator, and anyone who says otherwise is preaching a "false gospel" that cheapens the magnitude of the Love and creativity of God. Any time we find ourselves asking whether or not someone "belongs" in our communities, we can be certain that we have stepped firmly outside of the realm of the gospel and have started down a path that leads to destruction— not simply of those we exclude, but also of ourselves.

---

7   E.M. Seidel, et al., "The Impact of Social Exclusion vs. Inclusion on Subjective and Hormonal Reactions in Females and Males," *Psychoneuroendocrinology,* Dec. 2013, www.ncbi.nlm.nih.gov/pmc/articles/PMC3863951/ (last accessed March 5, 2017).

8   Sian Beilock, "Dealing with the Pain of Social Exclusion," *Psychology Today,* March 7, 2012, www.psychologytoday.com/blog/choke/201203/dealing-the-pain-social-exclusion.

9   Dominic Abrams, et al., "The Social Psychology of Inclusion and Exclusion," *Research Gate,* Jan., 2005, www.researchgate.net/profile/Dominic_Abrams/publication/226768407_The_Social_Psychology_of_Inclusion_and_Exclusion/links/56b4903008ae8cf9c25b8dcf/The-Social-Psychology-of-Inclusion-and-Exclusion.pdf++.

True inclusion demands that we recognize that only in our diversity do we more perfectly reflect the divinity of our expansive Creator. Whenever we are compelled to declare that someone doesn't belong, whether it's because of their sexuality, ethnicity, background, beliefs, political affiliation, disruptiveness, neediness, inconvenience, struggles, immaturity, etc., we are dehumanizing ourselves and the one(s) we are excluding. That is an assault on the very image and likeness of God in the world. We are attempting to cut off a unique incarnation and manifestation of the beauty of God, simply because we do not agree, do not feel comfortable, or don't know how to interact with such a person. But our discomfort is never an excuse to marginalize or exclude. In fact, discomfort is a sign that we are being called to go deeper, to do the hard work of getting to know another person, and to work on our own shadows that predispose us to discriminate.

The Results of Exclusion

All discrimination and exclusion is rooted in our own unhealed wounds or prejudices. We discriminate and exclude based on false narratives we've been taught. Those false narratives often put the unfair blame for our own pain or the struggles of our society on a person or group of people. They scapegoat. Unsurprisingly, the LGBT+ community has often been a scapegoat, not just for Christians, but for society as whole. In the early 1980s, the Central Intelligence Agency of the United States wouldn't allow LGBT+ people to work for the agency because of fears that their "perversion" would result in the downfall of the agency. As recently as 2017, the United States military has embraced discriminatory practices against LGBT+ individuals, saying, most recently, that trans* individuals[10] are "disruptive."[11] And who can forget the prominent evangelical televangelists throughout history who have blamed LGBT+ people for everything from hurricanes to terrorist attacks?

10 Trans* is a modern and inclusive way to write about transgender and gender nonconforming individuals.
11 Laurel Wamsley,"Trump Says Transgender People Can't Serve in Military," NPR, 26 July 2017, www.npr.org/sections/thetwo-way/2017/07/26/539470211/trump-says-transgender-people-cant-serve-in-military.

While these examples might seem extreme, they are a symptom of a pervasive distortion that runs deep in the human psyche. We discriminate because we subconsciously buy into the scapegoating narrative. That narrative puts the blame for our problems on anyone but ourselves, and then suggests that if we could only get rid of such people, our problems would go away. Of course, this narrative is fundamentally false. Nonetheless, all of us, in some way or another, buy into it. The problem is always the "other people" who don't look like, act like, believe like, or love like us. What can we do when we sense ourselves falling into this scapegoating mentality? We can remind ourselves that the problem is never simply *another* group of people, but more often than not the powers and systems that have been created in our consciousness by generations of diverse peoples.[12] This is what the apostle Paul was getting at when he wrote: "For our struggle isn't against flesh and blood people, but against powers, principalities, and dark forces in the unseen realms" (Eph. 6:12).

The forces that cause our most significant problems as a human family are far more insidious than *one group* of people. Getting rid of those people won't get rid of the problem. Most of our problems are fundamentally *human* problems, not racial, ethnic, religious, social, or sexual. They're problems that we, as a species, must come together to address in the midst of all of our diversity, rather than falling into the archaic, tribalistic mindset that causes us to go to war with one another, believing that this will somehow solve our problems.

When the LGBT+ community (or any other community) is excluded from the Church, we as the Church are buying in to this scapegoating narrative that dehumanizes both the excluded and excluders. We reveal that our true motivations are coming from a place of fear, which causes us to revert to lower, tribalistic levels of human consciousness. And when we function from fear, we are not doing the work of God, for the scriptures proclaim: "God is love and love casts out all fear" (1 Jn. 4:18). Such love propels us towards inclusion and unity.

---

12   Such mimetic theory was explored most thoroughly by French anthropologist René Girard. For more information, see *The Scapegoat*.

When we are connected to God, we are functioning in love, and love expels any fear we might have about one another, bringing us together. And when we commit to pursue life together, in community, with those who are different, we amplify and enable the supernatural power of love to heal and transform our lives and our world through us. This work will be hard and it will require much grace. But at the end of the day, all of us will become more human and will have further humanized one another. This is what it means to be saved, after all. To be "conformed to the image of Christ" (Rom. 8:29) is to be refined and reformed into the image of the "second" and true *adam*, the Hebrew word meaning "human." In Christ, the walls that divide us are torn down and we are united across all of the boundaries and borders that separate us, creating "one new humanity" (Eph. 2:15, NIV).

This is the only hope for humanity. Unless we are willing to do the hard, painful work of sanctifying and reforming ourselves through extending grace, welcome, and *unconditional love* to our friends, our neighbors, and even our enemies, we can never truly be conformed and transformed into the people and the communities that we are called to be. And as long as the Church continues to function in a way that excludes, demonizes, and marginalizes *any* community, we are pushing ourselves further from God, and perpetuating the "dark forces" (Eph. 6:12) that are at the heart of *all* of our world's problems. In excluding, we become the very ones of whom we are seeking to rid ourselves and we become agents of death and destruction, which is the greatest of sins.

2

Missing the Mark

One would be hard pressed to find any mainstream faith community that *doesn't* strive to be a community that welcomes and includes all people, regardless of labels or identifiers. Walk down any city street, and you will see dozens of churches with signs out front that proclaim, "ALL ARE WELCOME HERE." But many within the LGBT+ community (and many other communities) have found that the word "welcome" (or "inclusive") means very different things to different people.

This is why I think it's imperative to begin any conversation about inclusion by understanding what true inclusion is *not*. Because, unless we do the hard work of identifying all of the ways that faith communities and individuals have misappropriated inclusivity or taken a shortcut and only shallowly embraced "everyone," we can never understand why it's so vital for all communities to keep the inclusion conversation at the center of every aspect of their life and ministry.

In this chapter, I am going to go through a list of actions, words, and symbols that faith communities have used as proof of their inclusivity, and explain why I believe these fall short of the true inclusion that our Christian faith demands of us.

• Saying "All Are Welcome"

Many churches believe that they are welcoming to all people. They desire, in theory, to be a place where all people can come and be included into a community as they journey in faith. The problem is that the language of "welcome" is vague and hard to decipher. Many churches invite everyone to enter their building, but would have problems if certain types of people participated fully in worship. For instance, many communities would find it problematic if a bad-mannered person experiencing homelessness came in at the beginning of a worship service. Is that person truly welcome to be a part of the church, then? Or, what if a gay couple entered, holding hands and perhaps sharing a quick kiss? Would they be treated as warmly as everyone else? Moreover, many churches have requirements about who can participate in certain elements of worship, such as communion. Could that gay couple, the individual experiencing homelessness, or a nonbeliever be able to participate like everyone else in the service? If the answer is "no," then that church's welcome sign is deceptive and will likely result in a great deal of discomfort and frustration from a host of potential visitors to that church.

Beyond these examples, the other common meaning of "All Are Welcome" is that all are welcome—to come and change the way they think, act, or believe, in order to align with the worldview of those already inside. This sort of welcome is common among churches both on the right and the left, and represents a lack of tolerance for theological, political, or social views and practices different from the community's. Countless churches say that they "welcome" LGBT+ people, but when we show up, we find out that we are only welcome to attend the service and maybe a small group Bible study, but our whole selves are not truly accepted and the expectation is that we will need to *change* our lives before we can truly be included into the community. This form of "welcome" is nothing short of deceptive, but it's been accepted as a common practice among a great many of communities of faith.

If your welcome is not a *full* welcome that allows *everyone* to come just as they are—to participate fully, without judgment, and at every level—then your welcome is shallow and half-hearted.

• Not Taking a Public Position on Equality

Another common practice among moderate faith communities is to avoid talking about controversial social issues in order to create the illusion of being a welcoming and inclusive place for all. Many churches have chosen not to talk about or take a firm position on LGBT+ equality and inclusion in the public and ecclesial spheres, hoping to create a sort of "third way" approach in which all can live in the tension of disagreement.

The problem with this position is that it doesn't work in practice. A community where half of its members do not affirm the rights and dignity of LGBT+ people for theological reasons will never be able to accept that LGBT+ people are fully included in every level of life and leadership in the church. And, likewise, many LGBT+ people would not tolerate being in an environment in which a segment of the community or leadership actively opposed their lives and full equality in the church and society—and, frankly, they shouldn't have to be subject to such stress.

For a church to remain silent about LGBT+ equality and inclusion is to be complicit in our oppression. This is true for any other version of oppression as well. If your faith community does not boldly and loudly proclaim that you stand for LGBT+ equality, racial justice, against police violence, for the rights of indigenous peoples, etc., then you are aligning your community with the oppressors, and making it clear that the oppressed and marginalized are not welcome in your midst.

Now, let me be clear: I understand the impulse of pastors who are fully inclusive but don't want to say it publicly for fear of dividing or harming church attendance. Whenever a leader or community takes a strong stand on behalf of the oppressed, there will always be pushback and repercussions. This is seen nowhere more clearly than in the life of Jesus himself. Every time he stood for the marginalized, he was positioning himself against the religious and political establishment that had all of the power and the money. If he had remained silent, he could have avoided crucifixion and likely would have lived a happy life as a Jewish rabbi in Jerusalem. But the example of Jesus calls us all to die to our desire to be safe and comfortable, or to protect our privilege, and instead to give it all up for the good of those on the margins.

This is the vital choice every faith community and leader must face. Will you keep your large congregation, financial stability, and sense of security by remaining silent and avoiding controversy? Or, will you follow in the example of Christ and give up your privilege and power to advocate and include *all* people? To choose the former is to proclaim that you are *not* an inclusive community, and, in fact, that you are siding with the oppression of the community for whom you refuse to speak up. If this is the position you take, you should not expect any minority to feel welcome or included in your midst, because you're proclaiming the opposite of true welcome. If you want to include *all* people, you must be willing to put your budget and job security on the line for the oppressed, and you need to be willing to say that publicly.

• Putting a Rainbow Symbol on Your Website or Church Sign

There are many progressive faith communities that *love* the symbolism of the rainbow to declare that they're a welcoming and affirming community to sexual and gender minorities. Similarly, there are many churches that like to put up signs that say, "Immigrants are welcome" or "Black lives matter." These are great signs of solidarity and welcome to various communities that have been greatly harmed by the Church. But for many churches, these outward signs are the extent of their inclusivity. Often, these symbols represent a faith community that is out of touch with the current state of faith in the world. For many, these symbols do exactly the opposite of what the faith communities intended.

The rainbow flag is a historic and important symbol for the LGBT+ community. It is a banner that we have gripped tightly as a subversive declaration that we are out, proud, and unafraid to embrace who we are. For the generations of LGBT+ people who lived through the Stonewall Riots and the AIDS crises, this flag has a deeply important symbolic meaning. For them, to see a rainbow flag on a church building is a sure sign of welcome and inclusivity. It is a sign of healing and reconciliation.

However, for those born after 1980 or so (the "Millennial" generation and onward), seeing a rainbow flag on a church can often be a turn-off. The world in which this generation has grown up is one that has rapidly grown toward tolerance and even celebration of LGBT+ identity. It is also a world in which, because of social pressures, many churches have declared themselves to be "welcoming" to LGBT+ people, even adopting rainbow symbols to lure LGBT+ people into the doors, only then to tell these brave newcomers that the community was "welcoming" but not "affirming," which is simply a *more* damaging way to say that LGBT+ people are not seen as equals in these congregations.

Outward symbols do not always equal an inward sense of true inclusion, and many people have grown weary of the lip service that the Church has given the LGBT+ community.

Another reason the rainbow flag *isn't* necessarily a sign of being a truly inclusive community is, again, due to the differing experiences of Millennials and our predecessors. For those born after 1985, there is a growing sense that exclusively or overtly LGBT+ churches are neither necessary nor desired. As LGBT+ people gradually become integrated into every aspect of society, more and more people are expressing a desire not to be identified primarily by their sexuality or gender. Instead, they want to be part of truly inclusive communities in which all are genuinely welcome. This means that churches that identify as "LGBT+ churches" or are adorned with rainbow flags actually push away many LGBT+ people of faith; we want to be a part of faith communities that so authentically and holistically embody inclusivity that outward symbols aren't necessary.

Many LGBT+ people live our lives in spaces that are dedicated to our LGBT+ community. When we come into the church, we want to set aside for a moment the primacy of our sexual or gender identity to focus on something bigger than ourselves and to integrate into a community of people from every sexuality, gender identity, and ethnicity.

So where does that leave us? I believe that churches can tastefully integrate the rainbow flag into signage or church displays in order to show our desire to welcome the LGBT+ community. The key, it seems, is neither to rely on this symbol as the greatest evidence of inclusivity, nor to overdo rainbow symbolism in an effort to attract LGBT+ people. I recently preached in a church whose exterior door was proudly adorned with a rainbow flag and whose sanctuary features a *giant* rainbow stained-glass Jesus. After speaking in this church's worship service, a number of folks, both LGBT+ and straight, revealed to me that the rainbow stained-glass Jesus was a distraction that actually made them feel *less* rather than more comfortable in the space. It drew attention to one aspect of their identity, rather than welcoming their whole selves.

Please hear me: I am not *against* the rainbow flag or rainbow symbolism. But when it becomes the primary symbolism in our sacred space, I think we've begun to miss the point of why faith communities exist. The spirit of true inclusion is one that invites the full diversity of humanity into community so that we can learn, grow, and reflect the expansive, diverse God in whose image we are made.

In my church, we've incorporated a small but prominent rainbow graphic on our website that says, "Absolutely Everyone Is Included and Embraced Here." In our church building itself, there is no rainbow symbolism, just as there are no American flags or other symbols that separate us from the entire human family. Once a year, during Pride,[1] we pull out rainbow flags to celebrate the history of and continued fight for LGBT+ rights. Otherwise, our outward symbolism is pretty sparse.

• Having a LGBT+ Church Member

Recently I was having a conversation about inclusion with a well-known televangelist who pastors a megachurch in Georgia. He insisted that the church he leads is "inclusive" and that LGBT+ people feel comfortable in his community. To "prove" his point, he launched into a story about "a lesbian couple" that regularly attends his church, and who pulled him aside one Sunday to tell him how "grateful they were that he preached the truth and yet still welcomed them and loved them." What they meant by "the truth" was, of course, that LGBT+ relationships were sinful. The pastor's eyes gleamed with pride as he spoke about this token couple in his church, thinking that he had just trumped any argument I could bring back to him. Of course, my response was that this lesbian couple does not represent the vast majority of LGBT+ people in the world, and that even if they did, having *a single couple* in your church does not make you inclusive.

Now, this story is a very conservative example of how tokenizing a LGBT+ person could look. But many moderate and progressive faith communities—often led by heterosexual, white men—feel that they are inclusive because LGBT+ people enjoy coming to their worship service. Many of these churches avoid

---

1   "Pride" is a reference to annual LGBT+ Pride parades and festivals that take place in cities around the world to celebrate queer people and combat bigotry against the queer community.

talking about the LGBT+ "issue" at all, so that they can hold the tension between their nonaffirming members and their openly LGBT+ members. But let me be clear: having LGBT+ people in your church *does not make you inclusive.* The number of LGBT+ people attending says more about the individual LGBT+ persons' worship preference than it does about a community's fundamental posture of inclusivity. Yet many pastors and church leaders spend a lot of time trying to get some LGBT+ folks to show up at church, and when they do, they are tokenized while the church pats itself on the back for being "inclusive."

Inclusivity has far more to do with how LGBT+ people (and other minorities in your community) are invited into the life of the community than it does with how many LGBT+ people attend your church. If an openly LGBT+ person cannot (or does not) hold a position of leadership, represent the community publicly, or receive the *exact same treatment* as every other heterosexual member of the church, then your community isn't inclusive. And the truth is, any openly LGBT+ people in your community will likely be hurt and leave the church once they realize that they are not seen as equal.

Ask yourself this question: Does my church allow LGBT+ people to lead and speak publicly in front of or on behalf of the church? Would a LGBT+ couple be permitted to lead a marriage retreat? Would there be a question or fear among church leaders if any of these things happened? If the answer is "no" to the first two and "yes" to the third question, then your church is not yet *truly* inclusive. This doesn't mean you're not on the right path, for inclusion is a *process,* but that it would likely be more harmful than not for your church to claim inclusion at this stage.

• Having "The Conversation"

It is absolutely true that having the conversation about sexuality and gender identity in your congregation is a great start in the movement toward true inclusion. As you'll see later in our case studies, most, if not all, of the churches that I've profiled began by having such conversations—among the leadership, in small groups, and as an entire congregation about the theological and social ideas about sexuality and gender identity. But having the conversation is not enough.

As a LGBT+ person (or any other typically excluded person in your community), I can say that we do not feel any more at peace in a community just because the community is "having the conversation." The conversation is primarily for the benefit of the nonaffirming or not-yet-affirming congregation, not those of us who are excluded. That your community is willing to read a book, invite a speaker, or host an event doesn't make you an inclusive community. But it does make you a conversant community, which is the necessary *first step* for many communities.

At this point, I want to address a movement called "third-way," which has become particularly popular in the United States. Many of my friends are leaders within this movement, and I spent about a year advocating for the "third-way" position. "Third-way" simply says that a church has committed to remaining united in spite of disagreements, usually among church leaders, about LGBT+ inclusion in the church. These communities often *welcome and include* openly LGBT+ people, but cannot guarantee that they will not hear nonaffirming teaching or face nonaffirming sentiments. On the surface, this model sounds ideal for many communities. A church that remains united and in community despite deep theological disagreement on the topic of LGBT+ inclusion—great, right?

In reality, over the long haul "third-way" churches don't usually work, because either the affirming or nonaffirming position will dominate and push the other out. I've watched communities who loved each other deeply disagree severely over whether or not a pastor should perform a same-sex marriage in the church building of their "third-way" church. They wonder: Wouldn't that be a "church" endorsement of LGBT+ marriage? So I ask you: If the pastor doesn't do the wedding, are LGBT+ people truly equals in the church?

Even if "third-way" churches do survive, the problem is that the LGBT+ conversation is necessarily an ongoing conversation, and eventually people will get tired and leave—especially LGBT+ people: we've already seen the harm that nonaffirming teaching has on the mental health of sexual and gender minorities. It is neither healthy nor realistic to expect someone to remain in a community where their fundamental identity is always open for debate. And on the other side, as a truly conservative Christian, holding to rigid doctrinal boundaries, why would one remain in a community in which people are allowed to live in a way that you view as heterodox and potentially damning? People on both sides of the third-way paradigm will eventually grapple with these questions, and, more often than not, they will decide to part ways.

The third-way model is a great approach during the process of becoming an inclusive community, but it must be seen as just that—a *step,* not a destination. Likewise, if you're a part of a community engaged in conversations, it is absolutely essential that the folks about whom you're talking are a part of the conversation and have an opportunity to share their stories and guide the discussion. I've seen so many churches discuss LGBT+ inclusion and perpetuate stereotypes, misinformation, and ultimately end up keeping the conversation from resulting in any significant progress.

• A Growth Strategy

Here's the hard news: Becoming an inclusive community will likely *not* help your church grow. In fact, churches that embrace inclusivity will likely be smaller and have a higher turnover rate than churches that seek conformity and unity of perspective in their congregations.

Why is this the case?

Because a majority of people like to be comfortable, and very few people like to be challenged. It is far easier to be a part of a faith community in which we know what is expected, we know what to believe and to think, and we are solidly united with everyone around those beliefs and expectations. It's easy to unite people around a common worldview and common enemies, but it's nearly impossible to create long-term cohesion among tremendous diversity.

Think about the largest churches you know. Very few of them are progressive, inclusive congregations. If they are progressive, they're probably not very diverse and have created a theological or social framework that mimics that of more traditional, doctrinally based churches. Instead, the largest and fastest-growing churches in the world are those that value homogenous people, world views, and perspectives. They may express some degree of diversity, but they certainly aren't truly inclusive, because to be truly inclusive requires them to embrace a multiplicity of views and perspectives that fundamentally threaten the model that creates the cohesion they covet.

For the foreseeable future, truly inclusive churches are never going to be the biggest, sexiest, or fastest-growing churches, and I think we should be okay with that. This doesn't mean that we should stop doing outreach or seeking to bring more people into our community. Rather, it means that our goal isn't to have the biggest communities, but the most diverse and most engaged communities. A church of one hundred diverse, socially minded, deeply engaged people can have far more of an impact on a community than a church of ten thousand homogenous people, simply because the discomfort that is provoked in an inclusive space requires that we're poised to act on behalf of the needs of the various people groups represented in our communities, whereas homogenous communities tend to keep a safe distance from the real issues facing them.

Being inclusive also means that our churches must embrace a revolving door policy, gratefully welcoming newcomers and gracefully sending off those who leave. Some will come to an inclusive church for a season, during which they will be challenged and simply discover that it's far easier to be comfortable, and then they'll return to a more traditionalist church. Others will be provoked and grow rapidly through the opportunity to engage in living with various peoples, until they eventually find that church is no longer where they desire to spend their energies. They'll leave, not because of any problem, but in order to do something broader or different. Inclusive communities must always live with an open-handed posture, a posture of: "We're here for anyone whenever they desire to come and join us, and we are never angry when people move on." Resentment towards those who leave over disagreement only perpetuates an attitude of noninclusion, positioning the community to begin discriminating against people that remind them of those who have left, and stunting that community's ability to live into its communal calling.

In short, when churches embrace true inclusion, they are also embracing the likelihood that they'll never be the biggest church, the most organized church, or the most peaceful church. In fact, embracing inclusion is likely a call to the opposites of all of those things. Nonetheless, it's worth it—because, by embracing inclusion, we are leaning in to the deepest meaning of discipleship, reflecting the image of our expansive God, and creating a community that has true power to transform our communities, culture, and world. Becoming an inclusive church certainly isn't a growth strategy numerically, but it is perhaps the supreme growth strategy for transforming the lives of everyone who encounters your faith community.

When one embarks on the journey of becoming a truly inclusive individual or community, one is making a decision to embark on one of the most difficult and rewarding trajectories possible. Inclusion, while a universal human value, is also one of the hardest concepts to embody and live out in day-to-day life. When you commit to inclusion, you are truly committing to following the rhythm Jesus sets out for all of his disciples: the path of dying to self and rising again into a completely unique way of seeing and being in the world. It's a costly path, and one that takes a lot of work to maintain. It cannot and must not be a surface-level endeavor, or else the entire process will come crashing down. Inauthenticity never produces anything sustainable.

Now that we've explored all of the common ways that we may fall short of becoming a truly inclusive community, let's explore exactly what we mean by "true inclusion."

The Inclusion Imperative

Inclusion is the burning heart of the gospel. The moment those who bear the name of Christ embrace exclusion in any form, they have resolutely stepped outside of Christianity—they have embraced a *false gospel*.

Indeed, throughout the history of the Christian movement, many, if not most, Christian sects have abandoned the inclusion imperative that Jesus embodied and have embraced a diluted gospel message that limits the scope and the power of the work of Jesus Christ in the world. Why? Because embracing the radical inclusion of the gospel of Jesus is the hardest thing that any human being can ever do. It forces us to confront our ego, our pain, and our privilege, sacrificing it on the cross for the good of our neighbor, our friend, and even our enemy. To follow *that* call is the most difficult thing in the world, yet it is precisely the call of Jesus to all those who seek to follow in his footsteps.

This is why Jesus said the path that leads to life is "narrow" and there are "few that find it" (Mt. 7:14). This wasn't a pronouncement of the exclusivity of God's grace or love or saving work. Far from it: it was a declaration of just how difficult it is to comprehend, let alone follow, in the path of righteousness. The opposing road—the road of violence, selfishness, exclusion, retribution, and oppression—this is the road that truly "leads to destruction" and it is certainly true that "many walk upon it" (Mt. 7:13). This is why, in societies around the world, power structures that favor one class, race, gender, or religion and exclude and marginalize the others are so prevalent. It's easier to build a functioning society in that way. The rich get richer, the powerful are empowered, and those born on the lowest rungs of the societal ladder are told that there is nothing they can do about it—that is, until someone comes in the spirit of the renegade rabbi from Nazareth, proclaiming "good news to the poor," "liberation to the oppressed," and "God's liberating grace for all!" (Luke 4:18-19).

When the gospel of Christ unmasks the systems and structures of the world and reveals what they truly are—false constructions that are sustained only by myths and lies about the way the world works—then those on the margins are often empowered and energized to tear down the system and work for a society and a world in which all stand equal in the light and truth of God, and all are affirmed in their rightful identity as children of God, filled with the Spirit and empowered to be the lights of the world.

If this message of liberation and inclusion is the thrust of the gospel, what does that mean for communities of faith that organize around this message of good news and the example of Jesus? How are churches to participate in this radical path that leads to life? How are we to avoid falling prey to the false gospels that declare who is in and who is out of the loving and saving embrace of the Creator? Even the most progressive communities fall prey to the false gospel of exclusion. None of us is above the temptation to judge another human being, made in the image and likeness of God, as unworthy of inclusion or as fully and unconditionally loved by God.

The gospel of Jesus Christ is the most radical message ever heralded across the face of the earth, not because of its moralistic or dogmatic claims, but because it subverts the very way that humans are programmed to think, to live, and to love. This is why Jesus was arrested and crucified—not because he needed to absorb the wrath of God, but because he magnified the *agape* of God: the unmerited, unconditional, never-ending, ever-growing love of God for every molecule in the universe, without exception.

Jesus empowered the poor, the criminal, the minority, the irreligious, and the unclean. He called everybody to repentance, to stop walking in the ways that lead to death through separation, marginalization, and exclusion, and to begin walking in the rhythms of the kingdom of God, the *truest* shape of Reality that has consistently been suppressed by our own propensity to detest diversity and difference and value conformity. When the veil of deception is removed and the truth can be seen clearly, what is to stop those who have been kept low from rising up and toppling the ungodly systems of the world? And, likewise, what is to stop those at the top from fighting, even subconsciously, to keep the system running smoothly that privileges them but oppresses others?

If the message of the gospel is true, if a new way of seeing and being in the world is being manifested gradually over time, and if the truth of God's unconditional love, grace, forgiveness, and delight in all of Creation is being pulled up from our collective subconscious mind and embraced as the most fundamental fact of life, then the world must necessarily be fundamentally transformed. A death must occur, a death of egoist self, of our fleshly desires, which prefer to uplift those who have the same kind of flesh as us. A sacrifice must take place, not of animals or even of a messiah, but of our own comfort, privilege, and power. We must lay our lives on the altar of sacrifice, not to appease an angry God, but to demonstrate to our neighbors that we love them fully and that we will not live for our own self-interest but for the collective good of all of us, together.

To make this sacrifice requires faith, faith that the Spirit of God is actually moving humanity forward toward this higher level of being. It requires faith that, when we sacrifice our own privilege, we won't be betrayed by those around us and find ourselves on the bottom of an oppressive pyramid of power. And, to be honest, there is no guarantee that this *won't* happen. History shows us that more often than not, those who begin to awaken to the gospel way of seeing and being in the world often end up being oppressed, marginalized, or taken advantage of. It shows us that they are seen as naïve or threatening to those in power, and that those in power are happy to add another person to their oppressive structure in order to gain more power, more wealth, and more influence.

So *why* should we embrace this message of Jesus? Why would we sacrifice our own position of privilege and our own basic wellness just to end up being oppressed ourselves? Why would we put our *family* through that? It is far easier to continue participating in the world. It's easier to play along with the oppressive systems of the world. It's easy to delude ourselves into thinking that we're *progressive* just because we wave a rainbow flag in a pride parade, have racial diversity in our congregations, and use inclusive language in our liturgies, all while silently and secretly refusing to be *truly* inclusive, as the gospel demands.

What about the people who think, vote, and feel differently than us? Can we include those people as well? Jesus did. While not afraid to speak truth boldly, he also called his oppressors into the loving embrace of God. He proclaimed this loving embrace as the fundamental reality in which everyone exists, whether they believe it or not. Following Jesus down the path of true inclusion is the most difficult endeavor upon which any human being can embark. It is also the only path that leads to redemption and healing of our souls and our world. God doesn't call us to be *perfect* in conforming our lives to Christ, but God does call us to always keep stepping forward, allowing our lives to be refined through rebuke, learning, experience, and *grace*.

Grace reminds us that, even when we mess up, we're still just as completely loved, accepted, and included by God as when we're doing fine. Grace is the basis of our faith. It reassures us that even if we are rejected because of our pursuit of the kingdom of God, we will be led on a journey of healing and strengthening. When we have faith in grace, we can be confident that the Creator and Sustainer of all things is with us and in us, and will guide our paths. We may endure hardship, loss, and pain in the process, but grace promises that even then we will be provided for, defended, and kept in the love of God.

It seems naïve to believe in grace, especially to those of us who have experienced the full weight of the oppressive systems of the world or have lost greatly in following Christ's path. Grace isn't a guarantee that everything will work out in the end. It's not a vain promise that we'll somehow reach the "promised land" and see the full manifestation of the kingdom of God. No, to believe in grace is to believe that we are a part of a divine flow of the brave and the courageous who step out to fight and work for the more beautiful world we desire. Grace is the confidence that, even in the most painful periods of our journey, we are surrounded by a great cloud of witnesses who have gone before us, and whose efforts have made a difference in the world. Grace is the promise that our efforts matter too, that God will not let our lives or our sacrifice be in vain. And grace promises that God will hold and love us as we work to establish justice and peace for all.

Even though I believe all of that, that promise is not very consoling, is it? Anyone who follows in the path of Jesus is following a costly path. It brings sacrifice and pain, as Jesus made clear throughout his teachings. He constantly implored his disciples to count the cost, to understand that there was no way to follow in his footsteps half-heartedly. If they were truly "in," it would consume their lives. It would hurt. But it would also result in a peculiar, subversive sense of joy, peace, and meaning in life. According to Jesus, the way to live a fulfilling and abundant life is to give your life completely to the service of the world. It is to go deep into the depths of our true selves, tapping into the infinite love that is the very ground of our being, and moving from that groundedness with a message of inclusion, liberation, and a new way of seeing and being that is open to all.

This is what it looks like to follow Jesus. And the question we must each ask ourselves, at the very beginning of this journey, is: *Are we up for it?* Are we willing to forgo any and all privilege and power we have? Are we willing to oppose the dominant powers and people in our world and speak out like John the Baptist about a new world emerging in the midst of this one? Are we willing to dive deep into ourselves and deconstruct all that we've been indoctrinated to believe about how the world has to work, and then begin building a new world, right here and right now? And are we willing to be people of tremendous faith, trusting in the inclusive love of God and the power of grace to transform hearts of stone into hearts of flesh? Are we willing to lose members, money, and "influence" in order to be who God desires us to be? Are we willing to gain our lives by losing them?

I must admit I am hesitant. This call to follow Jesus is not an easy one. The path is narrow, the road is long, and the cost is nothing short of our lives. But I do believe that it is the best way to bring about the beautiful image described in the book of Revelation, where all people stand equally before the throne of God, in all of our diversity, with no fear, no darkness or tears, joining our voices in an everlasting song of peace. I believe that world is possible, simply because of the fact that we are able to conceive of such a world. I believe in the long line of prophets and pioneers who have seen a vision of this new reality and have run the race set before them. I believe that we are moving toward that vision, and I believe in the power of grace and love to save us from our propensity to exclude, marginalize, and condemn.

This message is the heart of the gospel of Jesus Christ, the cornerstone of Christian faith. Like Jesus, may we be willing to cross boundaries in order to welcome, affirm, and embrace every single human being. Like us, they are made in the image and likeness of God. They are our siblings, sharing in the same Spirit and Life that pulsates through all things. Unless we can accept this truth, we have no business calling ourselves followers of Christ

The Inclusive Kingdom

Growing up in a conservative Baptist church, I often heard sermons about the end of the world. My pastor actually taught an annual Sunday school class on the apocalyptic texts of the Bible. He would take us through the visions of wars and cosmic battles and tell us of how they directly corresponded to events that were happening in our modern world today. That, he said, signified that we had reached the end times and would soon be raptured off planet Earth and taken up into heaven, where we would finally taste the kingdom of God.

I remember sitting in the pews each Sunday, absolutely enthralled by the visions that he painted of the Kingdom—with its streets of gold, its crystal seas, and the throne of God beaming with an unapproachable light in the center of it all, beckoning us to revel in its warmth and glory, reminding us that we were home at last. That familiar image looks great in Thomas Kinkade paintings, and is how many people think of the kingdom of God. The other side of this image is not quite as glorious.

Those who are not welcomed into the kingdom of God, said that pastor, are instead crushed by Jesus' army of saints, who trample down Satan and all of his people (which is basically anyone who didn't agree with our particular brand of Christian theology) and leave piles of carnage for the vultures to devour.

This is what many people grew up believing the kingdom of God would look like: glory for the chosen and destruction for the "reprobate." But what if there's *another* way of understanding it? What if Jesus wasn't talking about the end of the world when he talked about the kingdom of God? What if he expected it to be a reality that we experienced here and now? What would *that* look like?

I'm certainly not the first person to pose questions like these. The belief that the kingdom of God is not some mystical reality to be experienced in heaven but a reality that Christians are called to live into and work to manifest right now has arguably become the primary belief of most Christians. Many prominent biblical scholars and theologians have called Christians to rethink what our Scriptures are talking about when they speak of the Kingdom. This is an important and urgent task for Christians, because our understanding of the kingdom of God has direct implications for what we believe and how we live in the world. I think we can all agree that the kingdom of God is our aim, the final destination, the culmination and result of our journey of faith.

However, if we believe the Kingdom is an other-worldly reality that is not going to be experienced in this life, then that changes the way we think and live. We will perhaps be less focused on working for justice in this life and focus solely on preserving others and ourselves for the life to come. On the other hand, if the kingdom of God is a reality that we believe we can experience here and now, and if we have a role in making it manifest on earth as it is in heaven, then the shape of our lives will be radically different.

What is key in either situation is having a clear image of *what* the kingdom of God actually looks like.

It seems to me that the best place to start to articulate our understanding of the kingdom of God is with Jesus. Throughout the four gospels, Jesus speaks of the kingdom of God (or "kingdom of heaven") about 105 times. (Yes, I counted.) It was one of, if not *the* central focus of Jesus' message and ministry on the earth. So if we want to get a good understanding of how Christians should understand the Kingdom, it makes sense that we'd look to Jesus.

In the gospel of Mark, we read that Jesus' first (and primary) message as he began his public ministry was centered on the kingdom of God. In Mark 1:15, Jesus proclaims: *"Now is the time! Here comes God's kingdom! Change your hearts and trust this good news!"* When Jesus talked about the "good news" (or "gospel"), it was inextricably linked to the announcement that God's kingdom had arrived. It had begun to be manifested on earth. It wasn't a far-off reality, but something to be experienced in the real world, right now. But Jesus was clear that it also wasn't going to be experienced in its fullness at the present time. In parable after parable, Jesus describes the Kingdom as a seed that is planted in the ground that over time will grow to full harvest (Lk. 13:18). This theme of growth and expansion becomes key to understanding the rest of Jesus' message and the history of the Church throughout Scripture.

In the modern day, we understand that everything around us is evolving. We understand that humanity has evolved over millions of years into the conscious agents that we are today. We know that our earth has evolved and is evolving. We know that our universe is expanding, pushing outward and progressing every second of every day. Reality itself is progressing. Everything has a forward motion to it. Growth and expansion are the fundamental realities of all thing in the cosmos, seen and unseen. So it's no surprise that when Jesus talks about the Kingdom, he talks about it as an evolving and progressing *Reality*. He said that the Kingdom would never arrive in some momentous fashion, but would grow into full manifestation, as it has been doing since the very beginning.

This message made many people in Jesus' day uncomfortable, as it continues to do today. We humans have a difficult time with growth and progression. We desire quick resolution and instant gratification. We prefer to think God will just drop the Kingdom from heaven and put an end to all of our suffering and injustice. For the Jewish people, who had faced nearly constant oppression since their conception through the prophet Abraham, it was understandable that they desired God to send a Messiah who would wage a war with and overturn their oppressor and would inaugurate a heavenly Kingdom all in one fell swoop. This is what they were expecting. This is what many Christians today are expecting. But this isn't what Jesus proclaimed.

Jesus talked about a Kingdom that had a lot more human involvement than was comfortable to many people. He taught, "the kingdom of God is in your midst" (Lk. 17:21b, NASB) and needs to be made manifest outwardly in our world through acts of justice, sacrifice, and love. In other words, if we want to taste liberation and justice, we need to align ourselves with the example and teachings of Jesus and work to manifest these things. It takes partnership with God. It takes obedience.

The earliest Christians understood this. This is why, in the book of Acts, we read of Christians developing comprehensive systems and strategies to address poverty and homelessness in their communities (Acts 2:44). This is why the apostle Paul spilled so much ink calling on believers to make their faith valid through service to one another (Gal. 5:6). This is why the apostle James said, *"faith without good works is dead"* (James 2:17). Inextricably linked to faith in Jesus is a life of service and action, a life that imitates the self-sacrificial way of Jesus, and manifests the kingdom of God through one subversive act of love at a time.

A Vision of the Kingdom

What does this Kingdom look like when all is said and done? What could our world look like if we all submitted to Jesus' way? How would our world be changed? How would our way of life be challenged? And where is all of this headed?

There are a few striking images in Scripture that give us a glimpse of what God has in mind for where all of this is headed. The most vivid and most familiar comes from the book of Revelation, which is an account of a visionary experience that a man named John had while he was exiled on the island of Patmos. Throughout the vision, John sees a number of apocalyptic images, which describe the coming destruction of Jerusalem and the redemption of the saints once and for all from oppression and persecution. At the end of the vision, John paints a picture of a renewed creation, one that has been liberated from the powers of sin and evil, and an advanced creation that reflects God's intentions for it.

In chapter 21:1–4, John says the following:

Then I saw a new heaven and a new earth, for the former heaven and the former earth had passed away, and the sea was no more. I saw the holy city, New Jerusalem, coming down out of heaven from God, made ready as a bride beautifully dressed for her husband. I heard a loud voice from the throne say, "Look! God's dwelling is here with humankind. He will dwell with them, and they will be his peoples. God himself will be with them as their God. He will wipe away every tear from their eyes. Death will be no more. There will be no mourning, crying, or pain anymore, for the former things have passed away.

For John, the coming of the kingdom of heaven, described here as the "New Jerusalem," is precisely what we see articulated in Jesus' life and teachings. The kingdom of God is not some far-off, otherworldly reality, but is instead God making his dwelling among humans. As God makes his abode on earth, all injustice, all pain, and all sorrow are driven away. John continues (verses 22–27), saying:

I didn't see a temple in the city, because its temple is the Lord God Almighty and the Lamb. The city doesn't need the sun or the moon to shine on it, because God's glory is its light, and its lamp is the Lamb. The nations will walk by its light, and the kings of the earth will bring their glory into it. Its gates will never be shut by day, and there will be no night there. They will bring the glory and honor of the nations into it. Nothing unclean will ever enter it, nor anyone who does what is vile and deceitful, but only those who are registered in the Lamb's scroll of life.

The kingdom of God is found in the midst of a sprawling urban metropolis where people of every ethnicity and culture, described as "the nations," walk in the light of Christ. We're told that the nations will bring their "glory and honor," which I believe represents the diverse gifts of each culture, their music and practices, the things which make each culture unique. The kingdom of God is a place where there is unity in the midst of great diversity, where we are not forced to abandon the multiplicity of identities that make us unique, but where the gifts that those identities produce are embraced and celebrated.

We are also told that nothing *"unclean"* will ever enter the city, which is a clear reference to the reality that John would have known in first-century Jerusalem. In the center of the city was the temple, God's dwelling place on earth, and the Jewish purity codes dictated who and what was allowed to enter the temple. Unclean things and people were not permitted. Non-Jewish people, who violated the purity codes of the book of Leviticus, were considered unclean. But the whole thrust of the gospel of Christ is that God has declared all of humanity to be "clean," a topic which we explored earlier. This new reality means that *all* people are to be welcomed into the Kingdom, regardless of race, religion, socioeconomic status, sexuality, or gender.

John's vision or revelation of the kingdom of heaven is one in which all people—of all races, tribes, and traditions—are welcomed into a new city, where they shall live lives of justice and peace in the way and presence of Jesus. What's striking to me is that this vision seems so incredibly "earthy." It's a city, not a garden like in the beginning. Our future there is not about sitting on clouds playing harps but living relatively normal lives in a society that is centered on the selfless way of Jesus. What we see is not a restoration to the way things once were, but a recreation, a completely new picture of what a perfect society for humanity looks like. It's a society in which everyone is included, all are welcomed. The gates of this city "will never be shut," implying that all are able to enter in whenever they please. As N.T. Wright puts it, "There are no locked doors in the Kingdom of God."[1] The gates of the Kingdom are open to all people at all times forever. Isn't that a great image of radical inclusivity and welcome?

The ideas that John articulates in his vision are not at all unique to him. As we have already seen, Jesus too casts a very earthy vision for what the kingdom of God is like. It's a progressively growing reality that will one day "work its way through the whole" (Lk. 13:21), transforming the world as we know it into a

---

1   N.T. Wright, "Scripture and the Authority of God: How to Read the Bible Today," in *Scripture and the Authority of God: How to Read the Bible Today* (San Francisco: HarperOne, 2013), 210.

place in which good news is proclaimed to the poor, prisoners are set free, the blind receive their sight, the oppressed are liberated, and the day of God's mercy is freely extended to all (Lk. 4:18–19). In other words, the Kingdom is the comprehensive restoration of all people to their fullest potential. It's also the radical unifying of all people across all of the barriers that divide them. In his final prayer before being arrested and taken to the cross, Jesus reveals his deepest desire for those who follow after him: "I pray they will be one, Father, just as you are in me and I am in you" (Jn. 17:21).

According to Jesus, the kingdom of God is a very tangible reality in which all people are reconciled and embraced, all injustices are overturned, and all of creation is restored. This is what the Scriptures mean when they talk about the kingdom of God—a reality that was expected to continue to progress and eventually culminate on earth as it is in heaven. It's an achievable reality, meant to be brought to pass by those who follow Jesus and his way. We Christians have spent way too long gazing up into the sky, waiting for the Kingdom magically to appear and descend to earth. But Jesus' vision for the Kingdom is even better than that. It's a new way of seeing and being, which is available to us here and now. It can be experienced today, if we open our eyes to the truest Reality that Jesus said surrounds us even now.

The Foundation for Inclusion

At the heart of Christianity is the message of a gospel that is "good news of great joy for all people" (Lk. 2:10) and a Kingdom "whose gates shall never be shut" (Rev. 21:25). This is a radically different message than what has been preached in a majority of Christian communities for at least the past five hundred years, and I believe it is the primary reason that so many communities of people have been excluded and denied their rightful place at God's table of grace. When we refocus ourselves on Jesus and the message he proclaimed, we quickly recognize the radically inclusive message about a radically inclusive Kingdom that he envisioned. Everyone, in all of our diversity, is welcomed into this new reality that God is creating *through us*.

The Importance of Inclusion

Not only is inclusion an imperative of Jesus' teachings, it is a fundamental human need, hardwired into our being from the time we are born. In the renowned psychologist Abraham Maslow's "Hierarchy of Needs," the need to belong is listed as one of the five core needs that is essential to the healthy development of human beings. From a Christian perspective, we can trace this need to belong back to the very nature of God in whose image we are created.

Within the Christian tradition, we have often relied on the image of a Trinity to describe the nature of God: three persons, sharing one essential substance, intermingling with one another in a loving flow for all eternity. We conceive of these three persons of the godhead as Creator, Christ, and Spirit, and believe that from this eternal intermingling emerges the very essence and energy of love. To love is to be in perfect union and deep relationship with another. In this Trinitarian image, Christians are proclaiming a belief that God is somehow fundamentally relational, and, as those who believe that human beings are created in the *imago dei* (or "image") of God, we believe that *humans* are fundamentally relational. To image or mirror our Creator and thus live into our full humanity, we must be connected to others.

This theological concept reflects this need to be included and to belong to a family, a community, and a people. When we are excluded or isolated from others, we suffer great psychological and spiritual harm. When humans are forced into isolation, we begin to lose a grip on our humanity and cling to the lower levels of needs on Maslow's hierarchy, caring only about safety and physiological needs, which makes it easier for us to objectify and be objectified by others. To live a solitary life, apart from others, is to live a less than human existence, and this results in the degradation of our psychological, physiological, and spiritual health.

So inclusion is no small thing. No, inclusion is about allowing others to live into their full, divinely created humanity, not degrading them, stripping them of their dignity and personhood. Framed in this way, inclusion is a value that every church and every individual should prioritize. If we're not helping others to become more fully human, more truly themselves, then why do we exist at all?

The Hierarchy of Inclusion

Because inclusion is such a fundamental human need, it makes sense that it manifests in multiple realms of our existence. For instance, while our most basic need is to be able to understand and embrace ourselves and our relation to God, this can only get us so far. For, to embrace and include ourselves, we need the assistance of a family system to help us to know who we are in relation to others. And that family needs to be a part of a community in order to form its unique identity. And if that community isn't accepted and included in the broader structures and systems of society, it will begin to experience the degrading aspects of being marginalized, which harms the community and the society as a whole.

These four realms of inclusion—*Self, Family, Community,* and *Society*—form a hierarchy of inclusion essential for flourishing. Each realm of inclusivity builds on the next, and, as each of us examines our own lives and experience, we can see how each stage has affected our own growth and development. Being excluded at any one of these levels creates deep trauma and the degradation of our personhood. For the rest of this chapter, I want to explore in turn each realm in this hierarchy of inclusion to help us grasp the all-encompassing importance of the inclusion imperative.

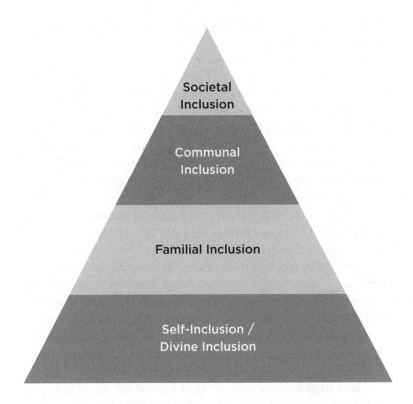

Self-Inclusion and Divine Inclusion

"How in the hell are you supposed to love anybody else if you can't even love yourself?" This famous phrase coined by the iconic drag queen RuPaul echoes the timeless wisdom taught by Jesus Christ himself two thousand years earlier when he said, "Love your neighbor just as you love yourself" (Mt. 22:39b). The key insight in each saying is that self-love is the vital prerequisite to being able to love anyone else. On the journey toward becoming a truly inclusive person or community, this is the often overlooked but absolutely essential starting place. Without doing the hard work of personal growth and development to become a person who is confident and whole in your true self, there is no way that you're going to be able to model or embody inclusion to any other group of people.

So what exactly does *self-inclusion* mean, and how are we supposed to begin working toward that?

This foundational level of inclusion is also paired with "Divine Inclusion," because to know ourselves is to know God, since our truest self and most fundamental nature is one with our Creator. In other words, each one of us is made of God. This principle is echoed in the opening words of the gospel of John, when the author writes: "In God was light, and that light was the life of all people" (Jn. 1:4). Do you see what the author is getting at? If you're alive, you share in the light of the Divine. This teaching has been at the foundation of Christian theology since the time of Christ, and yet, over the course of our two-thousand-year history, it has been buried beneath layers of distortion and false teachings that have served only to perpetuate exclusion—from God, from self, and from others. To be declared "children of God," as the New Testament echoes time and time again, is to be declared of the nature and substance of the Parent from whom we were birthed. This leads us to a profound conclusion: to learn to include and love one's self allows us to love God. And the inverse is also true: when we are cut off from our true identity, from a rooted foundation of self, we have cut ourselves off from God.

Can I truly include myself? Do I love who I am? Do I even know who I truly am? Do I comprehend who God has created me to be, with all of my quirks and uniqueness?

From the moment we are born, we conform ourselves to others' images and ideals. Instead of celebrating our uniqueness and believing that God has placed within us a divine identity meant to be explored and unwrapped as we mature and grow, we have viewed newborns as blank slates onto which we can project our desires and images, a ball of clay that can be molded into our image and likeness. And, to be sure, in one sense this is incredibly healthy. For, we understand our culture, our traditions, and the uniqueness of our familial tribe from those around us. These things are essential parts of cultivating inclusion at later levels of the hierarchy. But on the other hand, many of the identities that are forced onto us by our families and cultures have nothing to do with reality and, in fact, serve only to mar and restrain our true nature from being expressed.

Take gender identity, for instance. In a very real sense, humans are born with a biological sex based on the genitalia that we are created with: some have a penis, others a vagina, and others elements of both. But we now know that those body parts tell us absolutely *nothing* about the gender identity of an individual beyond the sexual capacities of the body and the hormonal compounds that will likely impact that individual as they reach adolescence. Having a penis doesn't mean that an individual is going to be attracted to women, play sports, or even identify as a male. All of those ideas are culturally rooted and are piled upon the fragile consciousness of young humans from the time they are born, often resulting in tremendous strain and trauma later in life when they come to realize that the person they've become is different from the true essence and identity that they experience.

My friend, and transgender theologian, Paula Stone Williams often says, "If you've talked to one transgender person, you've talked to exactly *one* transgender person." What she means is this: that the experience of one trans* individual is radically different and unique from the experience of another. I believe her statement is true not only for transgender individuals, but for all people. It's hard to live in the gray areas, the uncertainties. But each human is created as a unique being, and we would do well not to have expectations or requirements of who a person should become. We should allow ourselves and others to explore and express our*selves* in whatever ways feel most authentic and life giving, because in this freedom we most gloriously reflect the image of our God.

This is what the apostle Paul is getting at in his epistle to the church at Rome when he writes: "Don't conform yourselves to the image of this world, but rather, transform yourselves by renewing your mind in God's truth" (Rom. 12:2). Transformation is what it means to erase the masks and layers of false identity that we've accumulated and allow the light of God within us to emerge in all of its color, texture, and quirkiness. It means being who you are, even when the rest of the culture makes you feel ashamed or embarrassed about what that looks like.

Stepping into your true identity can be a hard process. It's also intensely liberating. And it's something that every single human is called to do. It is, in fact, the very process that makes us most human. For those of us who have grown up in family systems and communities that have forced us to repress our identity and conform to a constructed image, this process will take time and be painful. But the freedom one feels as one emerges from the restraints placed by society is incomparable.

Take the time to stop, look in the mirror, and gain a realistic understanding of who you are in reality. Whether as an individual or as a community, ask yourself: What are your attributes? What makes you unique? What defines you as different from other people or faith communities? What are the areas that you desire to see changed?

Such self-assessment is often difficult to do. It can help to reach out to visitors or others familiar with you and ask them to assess who you are from their perspective. Often, our perception doesn't match the reality. Taking the time with a friend or a psychotherapist to explore the masks that you've adopted over the years and remove them and allow your authentic self to emerge is a process that will forever change the quality of life you live.

In my own life, this journey has been a painful but rewarding one. As someone who grew up in a dysfunctional childhood home and then moved into a dysfunctional religious environment, I learned early on that I needed to mask my true identity, struggles, and desires in order to conform to the image of the person "God" desired me to be. After years of meeting with a psychotherapist (a practice I recommend to absolutely everyone), I have just begun to understand the reasons for the masks I've adopted, and have begun to distinguish between the false identities I've projected into the world and onto my truest self, which has lain suppressed beneath layers of self-loathing cloaked as spiritual righteousness. The result has been a life with much stronger boundaries, much more freedom to pursue my desires, and a lot less shame.

This is also why it's helpful for faith communities and individuals to engage in contemplative practices. Theologian William McNamara defines contemplation as a "long, loving look at the Real."[1] It's a practice that helps us step out of our false

---

1   William McNamara, as quoted by Walter J. Burghardt, "Contemplation: A Long, Loving Look at the Real," *Church*, No. 5 (Winter 1989): 14–17.

identities and masks, and lean into the *Light* that is our essence, our truest nature. From that perspective, all of our concerns, projections, and false identities fall away and we can experience the peace and bliss of simply *being*. This is how we are meant to experience all of life, but the disease of disintegration has so infected the human family that we now must work fiercely and consistently to regain this natural state of being, rooted in a deep love and appreciation of our true self and the God in whose image we've been fashioned.

This foundation of self-inclusion is the essential starting place for each and every person and community on the journey to living a whole life and toward embracing true inclusion.

Familial Inclusion

In the LGBT+ Christian world, one of the most heartbreaking realities is when children are kicked out of their family homes because they have decided to embrace their queer sexuality or gender identity. Studies have consistently shown that LGBT+ youth raised in conservative religious environments are more likely to end up homeless, and when such rejection happens, there is often a quick spiral into drugs, unprotected sex, and suicide. One of the primary reasons that these youth turn to such substances and practices is the mental trauma of being rejected for one's fundamental identity by the very persons meant to foster one's development and provide for one's needs. To be rejected by one's family is to suffer incomparable psychological harm.

The inverse here is also true. A healthy and nurturing family environment is one of the key factors that help a person to flourish. Because humans are fundamentally relational, and because we require nourishment when we enter the world, it makes sense that families developed as a way to help give us the training wheels we need to embark on the journey of life. Throughout the entire course of our lives, family is meant to be a constant source of support, a safety net and source of basic security throughout the highs and lows of our lives. When we have the support and security of a healthy family system, we are primed to tackle the difficulties of life with confidence.

Our culture is having a crisis of family, and so the fundamental wellbeing of society is also in crisis. That family crisis is a result of a rapidly shifting culture, in which the values and perspectives that one generation embraced have so dramatically shifted by the next generation that conflict and severe relational fracture result. In a healthy, inclusive family environment, these fractures are a normal, healthy part of family life and can quickly be repaired. But in a dualistic and polarized world, families not already practiced in being inclusive often fracture, splinter, and divide into opposing factions. And when families fracture, no one walks away unscathed.

For us as individuals and church communities, the work of fostering inclusive families is an essential task for the flourishing of the whole. Families exist to help each member's true self unfold in a supportive, celebratory environment, and to call forth the core values that each of us has "written on our hearts," as the Hebrew Bible declares (e.g., Deut. 6:6, Jer. 31:3). The family is the incubator of development and the cushioning beneath the surface of our lives, meant to catch us when we fall. Families are the key groups that get to see the full development of one another—the explorations, the mistakes, and the solidifying of identity in each person. The goal of a family is to celebrate each member's uniqueness. When a child explores their identity in the multitude of ways that they inevitably will, the role of the family is to ask questions, to support, and, ultimately, to celebrate the identity that emerges from the developmental cocoon.

The family is the gymnasium where we are free to practice and explore our truest self before we step out into the rough-and-tumble world. If a family is constantly demanding that one of its members live up to some idealized standard, some imaginary expectations, or some unrealized dreams of other members, they stunt that person's developmental growth and true identity and cause deep psychological and spiritual harm. If an individual does not feel secure at this most basic level, they will have a hard time blossoming in the other contexts of the inclusivity pyramid.

Families are made of imperfect and flawed individuals, and very few of us grow up in a totally supportive environment. Those persons whose identities the family unit saw as so outrageous that it cast them out will create a substitute family unit out of another group of people. This is essential.

Right after college, after I came out as gay, I was living in Washington, D.C., and began spending time in queer spaces that could help me celebrate and express the gay aspect of my identity. Immediately, I began to notice what at first seemed like an odd trend, but in retrospect makes perfect sense. Within the LGBT+ community, there were small groups of people that functioned essentially as *family*. Many of them would rent a large house together, do meals together, and spend holidays together, just like a "traditional" family. Many of the people I encountered had little to no relationship with their families of origin. Their families had rejected them because of their sexuality or gender identity, and, in the face of such rejection, they formed other cohesive clusters of support.

Whether or not the family of origin ends up being inclusive, each of us will find and create a family support system. It's a human need to know that we are secure, loved, and accepted. When we are able to cultivate this sort of inclusive environment, we prepare each other to move outward into the broader world with confidence and grace.

Communal Inclusion

Everyone desires a sense of community, a sense of belonging to something bigger than themselves. They long to be connected to an ecosystem of diverse people who offer them different perspectives, experiences, and friendship. Community is defined as "a group of people living in one particular place or having a particular characteristic in common."[2] From the earliest days of humanity, families who lived in one geographical region found that their lives were improved by cooperating with other families in another region, sharing resources and traditions—and also mating. As communities grew, they formed their own customs, languages, rites, and traditions that made them distinct from other clusters of families around, and they developed into unique cultures of their own.

---

2   *Oxford Dictionary.*

In one sense, it is impossible to have a totally inclusive community, or a totally inclusive family. There are particular factors that draw individuals and families together in the first place and make them distinct from others. To be a part of the Robertson family, for instance, means that you have to have been born into, married into, or adopted into our particular family grouping. It wouldn't make sense to call a family "the Robertsons" and then invite all people to be a part of it. Likewise, when communities form, there is always a core unifier that draws folks together.

The church I pastor, for instance, identifies as a progressive, inclusive, Christian community. While we strive to be inclusive of all races, religions, classes, cultures, sexualities, and gender identities, the reality is that if you don't live in San Diego, if you don't identify with our core values, or if you don't particularly care for Jesus, it doesn't make a lot of sense for you to be a part of our community. Of course, we will welcome anyone and everyone to our gatherings, but to become an integral part of this functioning communal ecosystem, you probably should be on board with our general ethos.

Another example is the San Diego Gay Men's Chorus in which I sing. Our artistic director always says, "You don't have to be gay to be in our chorus, but you should be gay friendly." His humorous point goes to the heart of the tension between community and inclusivity. It wouldn't make sense for a Gay Men's Chorus to welcome homophobic, anti-LGBT+ activists to be a part of it. That would threaten the very identity and ethos of the community. Nonetheless, striving for inclusivity as a community requires us to open wide the gates to anyone who desires to come, adopting a posture of empathic understanding (a topic we will cover in depth later), and holding a space for tension and exploration. If we believe that it is in our diversity that we most clearly reflect the divinity of God, we must look and listen for how each person and perspective contributes to the whole.

There are limits to how inclusive a community can be. As we saw in the example of the Gay Men's Chorus, the first boundary is whether or not an individual identifies with the common ethos or identity that defines and unifies the group, or at the very least does not oppose that ethos and identity. The second boundary is related: whether an individual poses a threat to the flourishing of anyone within the community. Thus, it wouldn't be wise for me to allow white supremacists to attend my church wearing Nazi paraphernalia, or to welcome vehemently homophobic persons to our Chorus. Anyone who opposes a *person* or group of *people* should not be included in an inclusive community. The inclusion of the exclusive destroys the entire fabric of an inclusive community.[3]

This idea makes many progressive people uncomfortable, and it's probably not what you'd expect to find in a book about radical inclusion. But welcoming those who oppose the very personhood or way of being of others in our community actually undoes the entire grounding of these systems of true inclusion.

I've also found that "size matters." The degree to which a church or social club can embrace inclusion is less than a neighborhood or city. Typically, the larger the group or the space, the more diversity can be held and celebrated. In a smaller group, such as a church, inclusivity is limited to the common core around which the community is organized.

Yet we are also called to live into tension as communities, to be willing to remain committed to *people* over the ideas they have or beliefs they espouse. This is why the apostle Paul exhorted the church at Ephesus to realize that their conflicts were not about "flesh and blood, but powers and principalities in other realms" (Eph. 6:12). Paul distinguishes between the people who represent ideas and the powers behind the people themselves. When someone enters into our space with a completely different world view or way of being, we often respond with a posture of defense, ready to attack or kick out the person if they speak or do anything we find offensive.

I believe the biblical call is for us to reject this posture of defense, by separating people from their ideas. This goes for us too, though I am a Christian. If someone disagrees with the beliefs of Christianity, their different belief, in and of itself, is not a threat to me. Now, if that belief begins to be manifest in physical action to harm or suppress me, this becomes a different conversation. But remaining conversant across divides, showing hospitality to all, and being willing to name our values and the

---

3   For more on the limits and dangers of including the exclusive, see philosopher Karl Popper's writing on the "paradox of tolerance".

boundaries that come with them is essential to living in healthy, inclusive community.

At the end of the day, our communities must work for equality and resist the impulse to become insular in our thinking and ways of being. While it is important for most communities to define their identities around a set of core values, beliefs, or interests, we can also learn to lean into the tension of welcoming the full diversity of people and perspectives into our communities, because communal belonging is an essential need of all people. The greater the diversity, the more enriching our communal experience becomes for everyone involved.

Societal Inclusion

The final level in the inclusion hierarchy is societal inclusion, which refers to creating a society and, ultimately, a global community in which *all* cultures, perspectives, and identities are given space to manifest and flourish. The United Nations defines an inclusive society as "a society that over-rides differences of race, gender, class, generation, and geography, and ensures inclusion, equality of opportunity as well as capability of all members of the society to determine an agreed set of social institutions that govern social interaction."[4] In other words, societal inclusion is more than a mere right to exist; it includes the right to have equal opportunity and a say in the development of the standards by which the society functions.

This is why it is so essential for LGBT+ people to have the same rights and protections as heterosexual people in society. The fight for equal marriage was not a fight to change a religious sacrament but a demand that queer relationships have equal standing and benefits as heterosexual relationships. It isn't enough that the government "acknowledge" our relationships if the government doesn't extend the same rights and benefits to them that other couples also receive. Inclusion is full integration into the life of a society.

When we get to the societal level, we begin talking about that other aspect of Paul's words in Ephesians 6. We can also understand the "powers and principalities" to which he's referring

4   The United Nations, "Creating an Inclusive Society: Practical Strategies to Promote Social Integration," (2009), 8., doi: February 24, 2018.

as the systemic forces of oppression that exclude and exploit certain types of people based on some aspect of their identity. Again, individual people may not actively participate in creating exclusive environments and cultures, but in many societies there is a privileged class that subconsciously participates in systems that are rigged in their favor and that operates on the backs of other oppressed groups of people.

This is how white privilege works in modern Western society. For centuries, white, straight, cisgender[5] men have worked to create a world that favors them, gives them positions of power, and enables them to amass wealth. As we know from a cursory study of history of the United States, for instance, the earliest European settlers believed they had a "divine right" to rule and reign over the "new world," and that they, therefore, murdered, enslaved, and exploited non-European people to accomplish this goal. With that as the foundation, the United States developed a culture and historical narrative that glorified the triumph of its European colonizers and perpetuated a myth of inferiority of all other peoples who were not white, straight, cisgender men.

To create a society that truly includes all people, such systems must be named, repented of, and deconstructed. That's far easier said than done. As we have seen in this history of the United States, we may think we have deconstructed the power of privilege simply because we give equal rights to others, but if the core of our prejudice is not acknowledged and actively worked against, its root of prejudice will rear its ugly head once again and fight to reinstate the "traditional" systems that favor the privileged at the expense of everyone else.

To create an inclusive society is to work for a world where all identities are seen as equally valuable, where all perspectives are allowed to be heard, and where only perspectives that hold equality and inclusivity as an ideal are allowed to govern. As my mentor, the renowned integral philosopher Ken Wilber, says, we must learn to "transcend and include," a principle that helps us understand how we relate to those whose perspectives are rooted in privilege and prejudice.

---

5   Cisgender is a commonly used term in conversations around gender identity that means that one's personal gender identity corresponds with their birth sex.

Society will always have those who are prejudiced and who defend their oppressive way of seeing and being in the world. We, of course, must find a way to allow such people to live in society. But we must also fight hard to prevent such oppressive ideas from once again becoming principles by which our nation and world are governed. We have to do both/and: both transcend oppressive ways of thinking and governing, and make space for those who see the world differently from us—while also preventing such perspectives from being able to be tangibly enacted.

This is why activism is such an essential part of any individual or community that seeks to be inclusive. Our inclusivity must extend beyond ourselves, our family systems, our communities, and cause us to work for a just and equal world for *all* people. Especially those of us who claim to follow the radical renegade rabbi from Nazareth are called to speak truth to power and work hard to ensure that inclusive and equal policies and practices are upheld in our society at every level.

• • •

Only when inclusion is achieved at each level of this hierarchy will we have taken the inclusion imperative to its furthest extent. Inclusion at each level provides the scaffolding for inclusion at the next. The imperative of the gospel of Jesus is to see the kingdom of God manifest on earth as in heaven, which means that we see the world reflect the diversity and complexity of God. Not to embrace the fullness of the diversity of God's creation is to fail to be faithful followers of Christ, and results in tangible harm and oppression. Inclusion is the burning core of the gospel, and its implementation at every level is the focus of our work.

The Problem of Patriarchy

Have you ever walked into a LGBT+ inclusive church and realized there is very little diversity beyond that of sexual orientation? Likewise, many so-called "LGBT+" spaces in society are often really inclusive of white, cisgender, gay men, but not so inclusive of people of color, non-binary folks, or women. This is where inclusivity and inclusion come to an impasse, an impasse caused not by inclusivity, but the far more insidious disease of patriarchy.

Patriarchy is a system of social order that privileges men as the ideal leaders and power brokers of society. The system of patriarchy, however, is not just oppressive to women. Because they are rife with misogyny, classism, racism, and homophobia, patriarchal cultures and institutions almost always develop a system of oppression that prevents women, an "outside" race, culture, or social class (usually immigrants), *and* effeminate, castrated, gender nonconforming, or homosexual people from rising through the ranks of privilege and power within the societal system. Instead, these classes of people become the wheels on which patriarchy turns, through forcing people in these categories to work and live in unfair and meager circumstances so that the "patriarchs" can live in comfort.

At its core, patriarchy is a system of "othering" that was developed to ensure that societies run effectively on behalf of the privileged. By and large, it is a system that has worked. The cheap or free labor of oppressed groups is, in fact, quite an efficient way to run a society. But that doesn't make it right or good. In previous periods of human history, this model of society has been taken for granted as the divinely dictated ordering of the world, and therefore accepted as truth by privileged people in most societies. But in the post-Enlightenment era, humanity is beginning to wake up to the inherent brokenness of this way of ordering our world, and is fighting for a new and egalitarian model of social order. Nonetheless, nearly every religious institution and government in the world remains firmly within a patriarchal structuring, preventing inclusivity from flourishing and equality from becoming our core operating system as people.

In our modern world, our version of patriarchy views cisgender, heterosexual, European, middle-to-upper-class men as the ideal of humanity and the rightful leaders of society. Though a majority of secular society may not outright embrace this definition, for thousands of years it is the system that has been embedded in our collective subconscious as the right and natural way to order society. In the church, on the other hand, this message has been boldly and dogmatically proclaimed from pulpits for centuries and continues to be the predominate model for ordering society, one that the Church has also deemed to be "right."

This isn't surprising in the least. As one looks through the Bible, it is easy to see that this patriarchal mindset has been dominant in the biblical worldview. From the earliest pages of Genesis, the idea that a cisgender straight man of a particular "chosen" race and socioeconomic status is God's appointed social and religious leader permeates the narrative. Women, non-Hebrew people, immigrants, and effeminate men are declared by the text (and, by inference, God) to be unclean, lesser, weak, and oppressable, creating a bold line of demarcation of who retains societal privilege and who does not. In an honor-based culture such as the ancient Near East, being seen as "penetrable" or "weak" was to be fundamentally oppressable by nature, and therefore race, class, gender, and sexual orientation were all fundamentally bound together in order to uphold the patriarchal narrative. This was not only culturally supported, but institutionalized by the Hebrew people in their Scriptures.

By the time Jesus arrives on the scene, patriarchy is well established in the Jewish religious culture, as well as in the Greco-Roman ordering of society, but Jesus himself seems to subvert the patriarchal norms. In the ancient world, to threaten societal norms would have been akin to declaring anarchy or seeking to overthrow the government. This is why Jesus was seen as such a threatening figure to the Jewish religious establishment—as well as the Roman government. But it seems that this was Jesus' entire goal: to threaten the powers that be and declare a new way of ordering the world. And when Jesus' life and teachings are read with an understanding of the patriarchal socio-religious context of first-century Palestine, many of the puzzling actions and statements of Jesus in the gospel accounts become astonishingly clear.

For instance, why were the Jewish religious officials so upset when Jesus reclined at the table of so-called "sinners"? On one hand, it is true that the Levitical law prohibited Jews from keeping fellowship with "unclean" peoples. But why? Because, the primary worldview prescribed by the Hebrew Bible is fundamentally patriarchal. For a patriarchy to work, it is essential that there are those who are declared "unclean" and therefore can be oppressed and forced to keep the cogs of the society running so that the privileged patriarchs can live with ease. Embedded into the Jewish consciousness of the first century was the longing for the establishment of the Kingdom of Israel: the glorious, idealized patriarchy in which a pure king would rule from the temple, the Jewish people would be gathered into one homeland, and the rest of the world would be excluded and even oppressed for the benefit of "God's chosen people." This is, understandably, for what the Jewish people of the first century longed. After being forced into captivity and oppression at the hands of other patriarchies for centuries, they longed for a day when they would at last taste the liberation that their prophets had foretold.

This longing was not at all unique to the Jewish people of the first century; every major culture and religion in the surrounding world embraced similar systems and desires. But when Jesus came along, he completely disregarded the purity codes and social standards in favor of a more inclusive way of being in the world. See, the Pharisees weren't mad simply because Jesus was transgressing the codes laid out in their Scriptures. No, their anger was much more profound than that. They were angry because Jesus' actions threatened the very liberation that they longed for, the chance to create a society in which they—the cisgender, heterosexual, Jewish men—would rule. This desire wasn't simply a selfish one, but one born out of years of oppression at the hands of other kingdoms and cultures. At a human level, the anger of the Jewish religious leaders is therefore understandable.

What's worse is that Jesus' disciples began to call him the "Messiah," a term reserved for the long-anticipated and prophesied king who would liberate the Jewish people and establish the "holy patriarchy" once and for all. If Jesus were *truly* the Messiah, they must have thought, he would have been working with them to establish a hierarchy that privileged Jewish men and put everyone else in their rightful place below them. Jesus was doing the exact opposite: he spoke words of condemnation against the religious and political leaders of Israel, and declared that the poor and marginalized would be the "greatest" in the coming kingdom (Mt. 20:16). In other words, he rubbed salt into the wounds he had created. Not only did he actively subvert the patriarchal ordering of society, but he declared that it was actually God's desire to put women, foreigners, the poor, and Gentiles in charge of the coming kingdom, not the religious and political elite.

When viewed this way, it becomes clear why the Jewish leaders wanted to have Jesus killed. His message was provoking the lower classes to organize around the idea that they would rule one day, and pitted them against the ruling class of society. When Jesus finally arrived in the temple, overturned tables, declared it to be a "den of thieves," and said that he would tear down the temple completely, the Jewish leaders were certain that his goal was to lead a rebellion against the hierarchal systems they had worked to establish, and that this rebellion could get violent. So they colluded with the Roman government that ruled over Palestine and convicted Jesus of blasphemy and threatening Caesar—both counts of which Jesus was *actually* guilty when viewed from their perspective. And Rome, as the triumphant patriarchy of the first century, was all too eager to bring a swift end to any resistance to their empire. So they convicted Jesus and sentenced him to death—all because he posed a credible threat to the patriarchy.

As Christian theology has developed through the ages, the reality of Jesus' life and teachings has been diluted. Theologians have gathered around the gospel texts and applied spiritual meanings to the teachings and events of Jesus' life that have obscured the cultural and historical context in which Jesus lived and taught. And while it is absolutely true that Jesus' teachings contained both spiritual and social aspects, the primary thrust of Jesus ministry was to inspire a people oppressed by patriarchy to discover their God-created identity as equals to all those who were in power over them and begin to create a world in which all people stood as equals, sharing all that they had and worshiping God without the need of mediators. It makes sense, then, that in the book of Acts we read of how the first Christians conducted their lives:

> All the Lord's followers often met together, and they shared everything they had. They would sell their property and possessions and give the money to whoever needed it. Day after day they met together in the temple. They broke bread together in different homes and shared their food happily and freely, while praising God. Everyone liked them, and each day the Lord added to their group others who were being saved. (Acts 2:44–47, CEV)

Do you see what was happening here? The early Christians began to establish an alternative micro-society that was truly egalitarian. They each had the same amount of wealth. They ate at the same tables together, regardless of class or gender. And they gathered together in the temple, the central place of patriarchal power, and conducted their own alternative worship services in which they declared *"Jesus is Lord,"* a radically subversive statement based on a common phrase used to pay homage to Caesar. In addition, the text tells us, "Everyone liked them," and every day new people were "saved." What was salvation in this context? It was liberation from the systems of oppression and the induction into a new alternative community, a new way of seeing and being in the world that essentially ignored the patriarchy altogether.

The reason the earliest Christians gathered together and did life in this manner was because this was *exactly* what Jesus was hoping for. This was what Jesus instructed them to do. For them, Jesus became the "alternative" Messiah, teaching them how they could live in the long-expected kingdom of God right in the midst of the kingdom of Caesar. Is it any wonder that the empire and Jewish leaders continued to seek to persecute and kill Christians in the years following Jesus' death? They had hoped that by killing the leader of this radical revolutionary sect they would kill the hope of those who followed him. But they couldn't. Because, once a person tastes liberation, it's difficult for them willingly to return to being oppressed again.

Throughout the rest of the New Testament, we see a continual wrestling among the apostles and early Christians as they try to figure out what it looks like for their alternative society to subvert the patriarchy. We see Peter and the early apostles struggle to welcome Gentiles, the privileged of the Greco-Roman society that the early disciples of Christ lived in, into their alternative community. We see Paul struggle to welcome other Pharisees like himself into the community. And we also see bold statements that show just how far these early Christians believed they message of Jesus should go:

> There is neither Jew nor Gentile, neither slave nor free, nor is there male and female, for you are all one in Christ Jesus. (Gal. 3:28, NIV)

> [Jesus'] purpose was to create in himself one new humanity out of the two, thus making peace. (Eph. 2:15, NIV)

The apostle Paul seemed to believe that the message of Christ was meant to extend far beyond the Jewish race and become the predominate operating system for the entire world. He saw that, in Christ, all social distinctions bowed to the common humanity of all people.

It also becomes clear that the great hope of the early Christians was that one day the egalitarian way of Jesus would at last become the way of the world. They hoped that when Jesus returned he would overturn patriarchy in all of its forms in every culture around the world, and establish one "Kingdom" where all stood as one. John sums up this hope in the book of Revelation when he writes: "The kingdom of the world has become / the kingdom

of our Lord and of his Messiah, / and he will reign for ever and
ever" (Rev. 11:15, NIV).

See, the fundamental thrust of the gospel is to overturn
patriarchy and create a new world right in the midst of this one, a
world in which everyone stands as equals before the only rightful
monarch—our Creator. It's a message about subverting the
systems and structures that oppress through acts of love, justice,
and resistance. It's a message of hope, which liberates each of us
to awaken to our connection to God and to one another. And
any interpretation that misses this layer is missing the primary
historical context of the gospel itself.

• • •

So what does this look like for our lives and our churches today
in the twenty-first century? Astonishingly, after two thousand
years, Jesus' subversive message is still as pertinent and offensive
as ever. And perhaps even more astonishingly, Christianity has
become one of the leading ideologies that perpetuates oppression
and patriarchy in the world. A few hundred years after Jesus' death,
when Emperor Constantine decided to endorse Christianity as
a "religion" and began to create holy sites, massive churches,
and shrines, he effectively stripped the gospel of much of its
subversive power and severely corrupted the message of Jesus.
There was a reason why Jesus and the earliest Christians rallied
around statements such as the following:

> The time is coming when neither in Jerusalem nor on
> this mountain will you actually worship the Father... The
> time is coming when the true worshipers will worship the
> Father in spirit and truth, and that time is here already.
> You see, the Father too is actively seeking such people to
> worship him. God is spirit, and those who worship him
> must worship in spirit and truth. (Jn. 4:21–24)

> After receiving the tabernacle, our ancestors under Joshua
> brought it with them when they took the land from the
> nations God drove out before them. It remained in the
> land until the time of David, who enjoyed God's favor
> and asked that he might provide a dwelling place for the

God of Jacob. But it was Solomon who built a house for him. However, the Most High does not live in houses made by human hands. (Acts 7:45–48, NIV)

From Jesus through the earliest disciples, there was an understanding that the temple and the religious establishment were not necessary to worship God. This was another aspect of how Jesus' message threatened the patriarchal religious hierarchy. Jews didn't need to worship God in the temple, but in spirit and truth. When the temple is removed from the equation, the door is open to everyone to worship God equally, without the need of a priest or hierarchy to mediate on their behalf. This is also why the only religious ritual that Jesus himself instituted for his disciples was that of "the Lord's Supper." This ritual, which was really just a meal that his disciples were to have regularly, was a radically subversive act, because in the Jewish consciousness of the first century, the dinner table was one of the most sacred spaces. Only those who were ceremonially clean would be welcomed to the table, and the ordering of the table mimicked the patriarchal ordering of society (hence the idea of the father at the "head" of the table, etc.). Remember that, during his life, one of the things Jesus was accused of was sharing the table with sinners and the unclean. This was a stunning offense because it threatened the most basic ordering of society. Thus, when the early Christians gathered at the table for supper—across cultural, religious, gender, and class barriers—they were literally breaking the most sacred of cultural standards. They were declaring the dignity and equality of every person gathered around the table. This is also why they used the language of "brother" and "sister": they understood that all of humanity was their family, that God alone was the father, and that Jesus was the elder brother, the example that they were to follow.

So as soon as Constantine institutionalized Christianity and gave societal privilege and power to the local leaders of individual communities (churches), it became a priority of those in power to turn this meal into a ritual that could only be done by an "ordained" class of "priests" on behalf of the ordinary people. As this simple, subversive supper was solidified as a ritual that mimicked a traditional sacrificial offering, its meaning was completely reversed. It became, not a celebration of equality, but a tool by which to draw a line in the sand and divide who was "in" from who was "out." Only the baptized, faithful, upstanding, "clean" people could take part in the ritual. Only those who believed the right things, lived the right way, and fulfilled the right prerequisites could receive this ritual, which was declared to be the very "means of grace" through which God's salvific grace flowed. Soon, the supper fellowship was transformed into the Eucharist, which has become a tool through which power, privilege, and patriarchy has been solidified and bolstered for nearly 1,500 years. I think it is safe to say that if Jesus entered a majority of "churches" that bear his name today, he would be flipping altars and burning vestments, just as he did in the temple two thousand years ago.

If our communities of faith are to be faithful to the teaching of Jesus, we must work to dismantle patriarchy in our communities and culture. We must work to create the alternative kingdom of God in the midst of the "kingdom" of this world, and seek to level the playing field so that all sit as equals around God's table of grace. Patriarchy is the principle enemy of the Christian, and is the primary threat to the inclusive gospel of Jesus Christ. Everyone who claims to follow Jesus, the renegade rabbi from Nazareth who posed a literal threat to both the political and religious establishment, must follow in his footsteps by flinging open our doors, dismantling our hierarchies, and giving the voiceless back their voices.

What does this mean in the context of our churches and individual lives? That, unless one is willing to work for the complete dismantling of patriarchy in our communities of faith and society, one is actually not interested in becoming inclusive at all. Likewise, if a church thinks it can welcome women but ignore racial justice and the LGBT+ community, it is fundamentally misunderstanding the problem and deceiving itself. Color, class, sexuality, and gender are all fundamentally tied together, and, to liberate one group, we must be willing to work for the liberation of all.

This brings us to another essential concept that we must understand as we seek to be inclusive: *intersectionality*.

Why Intersectionality Is Essential

Black feminist scholar Kimberlé Williams Crenshaw first coined the term "intersectionality" in the 1980s to describe her observation that race and gender justice were fundamentally linked to one another, and any attempt to address one without the other ultimately fell short. One of the examples that Crenshaw drew on to demonstrate the reality of intersectionality was the saga surrounding Anita Hill, an African American attorney who, in 1991, accused her former boss Clarence Thomas of sexual harassment. As Hill made her case, two opposing groups gathered to support her. One group was that advocating for women's rights, the other a group advocating for Hill's rights as a person of color. In the end, Crenshaw argues, Hill was forced to suppress her experience as a person of color in favor of being a champion of women's rights. In an article in *The Nation,* Crenshaw wrote:

> In this episode, the histories of feminism and antiracism were put into opposition, rendering Anita Hill a raceless figure that could represent either the puritanical sexlessness of white feminism or the universal figure of female oppression. Within the African-American community, arguments that sexual harassment was a product of white sexual discourse and that lynching symbolized the essential character of racist terror in effect erased black women from the picture.[1]

In other words, in Hill's case, her experience of sexual assault was a result of *both* racism and sexism, not one or the other. But in the public consciousness, she was forced to choose to address either the racial side of the equation or the gender side. In the same article, Crenshaw argues that both are essential to understand Hill's experience and the experience of African-American women in general:

> At the core of conservative social policy about race are old ideas that link racial inequality to non-traditional family formation and its attendant culture of poverty.

---

1   Kimberlé Williams Crenshaw, "Black Women Still in Defense of Ourselves." *The Nation*, 29 June 2015, www.thenation.com/article/black-women-still-defense-ourselves/.

Marginalized in this frame are structural and historical forces that limit the upward trajectory of scores of African-Americans no matter how closely they stick to a male-centered script of family and individual responsibility. And while foundations, legislative committees, advocacy groups and others rightly address crises facing black men and boys, their mistaken assumptions that such interventions will simply trickle down to black women and girls obscures the gendered structures of race, romance and work that contribute to the inequalities that stretch across black communities nationwide.[2]

As we saw earlier in this chapter, the oppressive system of patriarchy stands upon the oppressive intersections of race, class, gender, and sexual orientation, and all of them are inextricably linked. To understand the oppression of any one group, one has to look at how the forces of oppression effect all of the identities connected to any one issue. To address only one facet of identity fails to address the actual problem. Thus, while Anita Hill became a figure for women's rights, the general public ignored her unique experience as an *African American* woman, an experience that differs tremendously from those of white women. Similarly, this is why the most severely oppressed people in our modern culture are trans* women of color—who embody *every* layer of the patriarchal oppression. In order to seek liberation for them, it is clearly not adequate to address their issues as either women's rights, trans rights, or racial justice. All three are linked together in their very personhood, and must be addressed together. Any approach that ignores the intersection of these identities leaves the trans* woman of color in an oppressive and exclusive environment.

To become inclusive is to work to understand the intersectional identities of individuals and to create communities and societies in which they are liberated in every facet of their identity. *The goal of becoming inclusive isn't to have "more interesting" or bigger communities, but instead is the salvation and liberation of every single aspect of every single person's identity so that they can be the person who God created them to be.* To be inclusive is to seek salvation and redemption for the world through the liberation

2   Ibid.

of each individual. To do so, we must understand the ways that the oppressive structures that we are seeking to dismantle work against the various intersecting identities of people. This means taking an intersectional approach to inclusive justice.

I can't tell you how many times I've sat down with pastors of churches to have a conversation about some "controversial" topic—say, women in ministry—and have eventually asked, "So how are you dealing with racism?" only to be told something along the lines of, "Race really isn't our passion issue around here," or, "We can only focus on one problem at a time." Both responses fundamentally misunderstand the problem they are trying to address, and therefore they will inevitably falter and harm the very people they're trying to include. If your church is willing to focus on gender equality—giving women and men equal roles in the church—then you must also begin to address racism, classism, and LGBT+ inequality. They're all connected. The theology one uses to shift perspective on one of these topics is the theological tool necessary to shift perspectives on all the other issues—because, the issue isn't racism, sexism, classism, or homophobia; each one of those is a pillar of a larger, more oppressive system of patriarchy. Jesus came to liberate us from the full weight of the patriarchal system, and, therefore, *we must work to dismantle all the systems at the same time.*

Forfeiting Privilege

In order to practice intersectional inclusivity, we must humble ourselves and listen to the voices of the marginalized both within and outside of our circles of community, willing to repent of the harm we've done, and willing to change our traditions, practices, and beliefs to reflect the inclusive heart of our Creator, no matter what the cost is to us. This is what it means to "take up the cross," after all: to be willing to name our privilege, willing to set it aside to feel and walk alongside the oppression and the suffering of others, willing to carry the burden in solidarity with them, and willing to destroy it through our own self-sacrifice.

The Christian tradition gives us a powerful image to understand just what this practice of self-sacrifice looks like. In the introduction, I referenced the apostle Paul's letter to the church at Philippi, in which he quotes an early Christian hymn that was recited in the first few centuries after Christ's death, describing the means and manner of Christ's sacrifice. These are the words of that hymn:

> [Christ Jesus], being in very nature God,
>> did not consider equality with God something to
>> be used to his own advantage;
>> rather, he made himself nothing
>> by taking the very nature of a servant,
>> being made in human likeness.
>
> And being found in appearance as a man,
>> he humbled himself
>> by becoming obedient to death—
>> even death on a cross!
>
> Therefore God exalted him to the highest place...
>> (Phil. 2:6–11, NIV)

In this hymn, we see the path of salvation through intersectional inclusivity. We are told that Jesus Christ was *"in very nature God"*—arguably the most privileged position in all of the universe—and yet he didn't exploit his equality with God to his own advantage. He knew he possessed power and privilege, but willingly chose not to exploit it to have an easier path. Instead, "he made himself nothing by taking the very nature of a servant," the Greek word here translated as "servant" being δούλου, which literally translates to "slave." In other words, Christ forfeited his privilege as God and willingly gave up everything to stand in solidarity with a slave—the lowest of the low in first-century Palestine.

But Christ went even further: he "humbled himself by becoming obedient to death—even death on a cross." Christ not only forfeited his privilege as God, he not only became a slave, he also willingly died in the most dishonorable form possible—crucifixion, a form of capital punishment reserved for the worst infidels and criminals. There is no more potent example of someone giving up their privilege so totally and completely. *because* he gave it up, God exalted him. This is the upside-down nature of the world that God is seeking to create, the world to which God calls us as disciples of Christ. It's a world in which those with the most power and privilege don't have to be forced to stop oppressing others for their own good, but, instead, willingly give up their positions and privilege in order to dismantle systems of oppression and level the playing field for all. In the new reality that God is creating, the most marginalized are the ones who hold true wisdom and the power, but the privileged are too blind to see this.

To be authentic followers of the example of Jesus means we must examine our lives, acknowledging the privilege we have, and leveraging it to benefit those who have been oppressed because of it. The call here is not to give "handouts" to those who haven't gotten as far as you, but instead to acknowledge that the only reason you've been able to get as far as you have is because you've been propelled forward at the expense of others. Until we acknowledge and willingly forfeit this privilege, leveraging it to level the playing field, the world God desires for us will remain far off and our attempts at inclusivity will fall short.

Sacrificial, intersectional inclusion is the only path to salvation, and the most fundamental call of Christ to his followers. The road is narrow and is hard to walk upon, but when we do, it leads to life and liberation for us all.

6

The Ingredients of Inclusion

Now that we understand inclusion, and now that we understand the mechanisms that prevent us from being inclusive, I want to focus on a few of the key ingredients that are necessary for any person or community to start becoming inclusive.

The Slippery Slope

After spending years consulting with church leaders who are heading toward inclusion, I have come to the realization that what most perpetuates exclusion in the church is our theology, and specifically a theology that extols and perpetuates patriarchy. Yet many of us in the church believe we can embrace true inclusion while gripping tightly to a traditional theology. I am utterly convinced that unless we rethink *every* aspect of our inherited theology, we will never be free to become the truly inclusive people that God calls us to be.

Early on in my work for LGBT+ inclusion, I set out to prove to the evangelical establishment that I was a faithful conservative evangelical theologically, but had come to a different interpretation of the six biblical "clobber passages."[1] Everything else about me had remained the same, my argument went, so I should be welcomed back into the evangelical fold. In the earliest stages of my journey of inclusion, this was certainly true for me. I held on to most of the same theology that I had always embraced, fighting fiercely against any idea that becoming inclusive of women in ministry or LGBT+ relationships was a slippery slope away from traditional, conservative theology. All

---

1   The six passages throughout the Hebrew Bible and New Testament that speak to the concept of homosexuality in some form are often called "clobber passages" because of the way they are used to beat the LGBT+ community into conformity with the patriarchial, heteronormative standards of the ancient world.

of my conservative evangelical professors in Bible college had warned me of this, as if changing my theology would be the straw that broke the back of God's mercy and would condemn me to hell.

But after journeying down the path of inclusion, and after having worked with hundreds of pastors, theologians, and individual LGBT+ people on their journey to inclusion, I can say with confidence that to become inclusive *is* a slippery slope—just not in the direction my evangelical friends meant. Inclusion will require you to change your theology, time and time again. You see, at the heart of the damage the church has done by excluding and marginalizing others is an entire theology. The problem in this paradigm isn't a misinterpretation of six verses of scripture, but an entire way of viewing, reading, and using Scripture. The problem isn't misunderstanding isolated instances of Jesus' teachings, it's misunderstanding what Jesus came to do. The entire evangelical theological paradigm depends upon patriarchy, and to liberate theology from patriarchy requires a complete deconstruction of the entire paradigm.

Until you are willing to dive headfirst onto the so-called "slippery slope" and allow the wind of the Holy Spirit to guide you to new theological terrain, you will never be truly inclusive. To be an inclusive church or an inclusive person, I do not believe one can maintain a "traditional" Christian theology, one which believes in a God who condemns and excludes his enemies (even though he teaches us to love ours), one in which believing the right doctrines and conforming to a singular code of morality is touted as the key to salvation, one that insists that the patriarchal code laid out within the pages of the Bible is the only right way to order churches, families, and societies. Inclusion and patriarchy are mutually exclusive.

Oftentimes, this realization will not be apparent to someone in the early stages of their desire to be inclusive. But as we dig into the perspectives of queer theologians, liberation theologians, indigenous theologians, and womanist theologians, we begin to see the ways in which our theologies are rooted in the singular perspective of the European, straight, privileged, *man*. Logically, no theology that emerges from this perspective is going to resemble anything akin to the perspectives of the marginalized first-century Jewish rabbi whose words echo throughout the gospels, or the early woman who first preached the words that we now know as the book of Hebrews.[2] The Bible and our faith come from the margins. To be faithful to the heart of Jesus' teachings, how can we not be willing to allow the perspectives of the marginalized to inform and change our interpretation of Scripture?

I have discovered this for myself. When I began to listen and digest more marginal theological perspectives, and when I began to deconstruct and reconstruct an inclusive theology, I found that many people feel compelled to join churches and movements that dare to step beyond the boundaries of so-called "orthodoxy," and that many of them have rediscovered and recommitted themselves to following Jesus in more authentic and genuine ways. It is far better to deal with the root of our exclusion, which lies at the heart of traditional theology, than to try to inject moments of inclusivity into a paradigm that is fundamentally exclusive.

The slippery slope is real. But when we dare to venture down it, we are taking the road of authentic faith. When our faith causes us to question the opinions of those in power, we know that we are walking in the footsteps of Jesus. When our faith centers the voices of those who have been silenced for centuries, we can be assured that we're marching to the rhythm of the kingdom of God.

So embrace the journey, leaving no stone unturned, for nothing is too sacred to be questioned, and no one's perspective is too marginal to be considered.

This leads us to the next essential ingredient on the path to inclusion; I call it the *metanoia principle.*

The Metanoia Principle

If you grew up around Christians, it's likely you heard the word *repent* preached from a pulpit a time or two. And if you, like me, now embrace a more progressive understanding of theology, the

2   For more information on the female authorship of the book of Hebrews (thought to be a sermon of Pricilla), I recommend reading the following article from the *Journal of Christians for Biblical Equality:* Haddad, Mimi. "Priscilla, Author of the Epistle to the Hebrews?" *CBE International*, 31 Jan. 1993, www.cbeinternational.org/resources/article/priscilla-papers/priscilla-author-epistle-hebrews.

word *repent* probably makes you feel a little queasy. In traditional Christian language, the word *repent* conjures up images of begging an angry God to forgive us of our sins, and fearing punishment or damnation if we don't secure his mercy. It's a word tied to a theology of guilt that sees humanity's primary problem as the fact that we've "offended" God by our immorality, and thus are rightfully heading toward hell. If we take this understanding of the word and read it back into the gospels, we tend to see Jesus' entire message as being about repenting or perishing.

This version of repentance-driven theology can be quite abusive to the average Christian, and is the reason that many people walk away from the Christian faith. But for minorities— women, non-European people, and LGBT+ people, people with disabilities—the severity of the damage caused by the call to "repent" is amplified. For those in these minority communities, our very identities and nature are often deemed to be infected with sin, and the call to repent is essentially the call to suppress or to kill part of our fundamental identity. If you're a woman who is gifted with skills of leadership, and you try to exercise them, in many churches you'll be told to "repent," to stop, to seek forgiveness, and never to try that again. If you're from a non-European culture, you may be told that some of the customs your family embraces are demonic or evil, and you should "repent" and stop these practices. And if you're LGBT+, you're told that the very desire within you to love the persons of the same gender or to identify as anything other than your biological sex is an affront to God's ordering of creation, and that you need to "repent."

This theology of repentance is abusive and unhealthy because it imagines God as punitive, retributive, and unmerciful. No wonder that people who believe such a theology live in fear and trembling of such a God! No wonder their knees buckle under the weight of the demands placed on them by their so-called "benevolent" Creator. Their lives become unlivable. They become who they are not really, and the resulting trauma and anxiety drains the life from their souls. If this understanding of the Christian practice of repentance is authentic to Christianity, most of us would be better off choosing a healthier faith and worldview.

We must figure out another way of thinking about repentance. It's undeniably a part of the Christian Scriptures, but the way it's often understood and practiced produces death, not life. So what are we to do? Perhaps we've gotten repentance all wrong, and the word that we translate as "repentance" is actually a key practice of inclusive communities.

As is so often the case, what we have here is a case of mistranslation. The word in the New Testament most often translated "repentance" is the Greek word μετάνοια, or *metanoia,* which literally translates as "to expand one's mind." The etymological roots are the words μετά, which means "to expand or grow," and νοια, which means "brain or mind." Such expanding of our minds is essential for communities seeking to become inclusive. We must always be willing to expand our minds to embrace the full diversity of God as revealed in humanity, which also means being willing to rethink and reform our policies, theology, and structures.

Another way to think of *metanoia* is by one of the battle cries that emerged from the Protestant Reformation—*Ecclesia Reformata, Semper Reformata*—which means, "The Church is reformed and always reforming." It's ironic that the churches that most fiercely claim this tradition are often those that are most opposed to major reformations of thought and practice. Nonetheless, to be inclusive means to keep reforming.

Fundamental to the idea of reformation is a deep-seated humility, the understanding that we do not have the capacity to embrace even a fraction of the knowledge about God, or anything created in God's image or by the God's creativity (in other words, *everything*). To be inclusive means to give up the certainties of which religion often assures us, and to be willing to hold tensions, to deconstruct, and to experience total transformation throughout our lives.

The good news that Jesus proclaimed is fundamentally tied to our ability to expand our thinking, embrace more perspectives, and hold in tension the real, raw diversity of Creation. And in this space, the traditional definition of repentance comes into play as well. As we seek to reform and be reformed, we have to name our missteps—the ways in which we've participated in marginalization—and be willing to hear and accept the hurt that we've caused others by excluding them. This is where empathic understanding comes in.

Empathic Understanding

A few years ago, while I was consulting with a group of evangelical pastors about how they could move their church toward full inclusion of LGBT+ people, we came to a realization that has forever shaped how I engage in this work: that only through hearing the stories and struggles of LGBT+ people and doing the hard work of sitting with them on the margin do we both empathize with and understand the pain that nonaffirming theology and practice has on them.

Now, for most readers, this insight won't come as a dramatic breakthrough. Of course, it's only when we hear the stories and see through the eyes of others who see the world with a fundamentally different set of lenses that we can enact the process of reshaping our perspective. What's different about empathic understanding in this context is that it's not a one-time action, but an ongoing posture of life, modeled on the life and example of Jesus himself.

The Incarnation is the most profound model of empathic understanding in the universe. In the person of Jesus, God stepped into the world and experienced what it was like to be human. God didn't just listen to the plight of humans; God experienced what it was like to human—to walk alongside humanity and discover what the world was like through our eyes. Similarly, when I talk about empathic understanding, I am talking about doing the hard work of moving outside the walls of our churches and into spaces that those whom we claim to want to include frequent as safe spaces. Empathic understanding usually doesn't happen naturally; it's incredibly intentional, has no intended outcome, and is lived as a rhythm of life, not a one-time action.

Throughout much of Jesus' life and teaching, he remained outside of the synagogue and away from the temple, the two places that he likely would have felt most "safe" and welcomed (at least before his preaching became radicalized against the institution). These were also the places that he wanted to reform. However, Jesus understood that true and lasting change comes only in proximity to those who are marginalized and excluded, and showed us that such change must happen within ourselves rather than in those who are excluded. When we examine the development of the teachings of Jesus, we see a message that is shaped by the experiences of the "least of these," those for whom Jesus left the temple and among whom he spent his days.

This is precisely why those in power excluded those they saw as "unclean" and forbade those who were seen as "clean" from fraternizing with them: it ensured that the corruption of the system they had created to favor themselves wouldn't be revealed. They knew that, as soon as the voices, stories, and lives of the marginalized were witnessed firsthand, folks would see the injustice and rebel. This is what happens to Jesus and his disciples: the more they violate cultural taboos and sit with the unclean in their day-to-day lives, the more they are empowered to speak up on their behalf and to work for their liberation.

This is the power of empathic understanding. Once people see the impact of their empathy and intervention, no one can resist the power of stepping into the lives of those they have excluded and demonized. And yet, most churches and individuals never take the time to leave their places of comfort, authority, and power.

If you were to walk into the denominational offices of any group of Christians in North America, you'd more than likely stumble onto conversations about how churches can *attract* more people to enter their buildings, participate in their services, and, ultimately, give money to their institution. Very few institutions are having conversations about how to "do life" out among communities, in the world, beyond church properties or religious services. Very few institutions are thinking about ways in which they can open up their properties to become hubs in which the community can use their space, rather than focusing on how their church can maximize it.

Yet Jesus never stayed in the place of power. Instead, he helped people enter into life abundant wherever they were located. Whereas, at the heart of most institutional religion is the desire to create conformity to the institution, Jesus never demanded such conformity, but met people where and how they were.

What if our faith communities were to become touch-points: places where folks can come together to learn, provoke one another, and organize—but then intentionally pushed people out away from the institution to tend to the needs, desires, and interests of communities and cultures beyond those faith communities? What if local faith communities were to uplift and empower local leaders to lean into their dreams and callings, and give them resources to host events and programs from their own perspectives and worldviews? And what if those connected to the faith community showed up to support, to learn, to participate— instead of to control or to lead?

What would emerge would be empathic understanding. Inviting those who otherwise wouldn't be a "member" of our traditional faith community to find there the resources, the platform, and the ability to express themselves would help us all learn and grow. It would give us the opportunity to see the world from another's perspective. And it would model the example of Jesus, who infused his vision for the kingdom of God into everything he did—whether joining "immoral people" for a dinner party, discussing spirituality with peasants on the mountainside, or even occasionally entering the institution to stir things up.

Through Jesus' constant contact with diverse groups of people, his own perspective was refined and shaped. Such growth occurs only through contact with the perspectives and experiences of others. If we want to become communities that value empathic understanding, we must spend most of our energy out *in* the world, not seeking to entice people to enter into our communities.

What does this look like in real life?

Well, for many of those evangelical pastors who became inclusive, it began by leaving their comfort zones and entering LGBT+ spaces. One of my friends, a former Southern Baptist Pastor, Danny Cortez, tells how much of his journey toward inclusion happened because he began spending hours every week writing his sermons in a coffee shop in West Hollywood, a LGBT+ neighborhood in Los Angeles. He began to meet people, make friends, hear stories, and recognize the damage that people like him had done to those in that community. After that, his perspective began to change. His worldview expanded. And he shifted the way he preached, believed, and lived.

Empathic understanding means truly being able to identify with another's perspective and respond in kind. It requires humility: the realization that one doesn't have it all figured out, but rather has far more to learn than to teach. It requires that we consider others above ourselves, as the apostle Paul writes (Phil. 2:3). When these values become the values of our community, then the way we "do" church changes fundamentally. The ways in which we "do" life change fundamentally. We lose a sense of stability and equilibrium, but we gain the ability to grow and to empower others to grow as well.

Becoming a community of empathic understanding isn't going to grow your church. If you lean into this model, you are unlikely to find hundreds or thousands of people showing up for Sunday worship. But your community will be connected to, and cultivating, growth and wholeness for people in your community who may never set foot in a traditional worship service. Isn't this the situation that Jesus would desire—one of mutual growth, mutual empowerment, and tangible transformation of communities for the common good of absolutely everyone?

Bigger Than Any One Minority Group

One evening, I was sitting in a room of straight, white, progressive pastors who were talking about how they first came to the churches that they were now pastoring. One by one, this group of *straight* men recounted to me how they went to a popular LGBT+ church database (GayChurch.com) to look for communities of which they wanted to be a part. Intrigued, I pressed for an explanation as to why they used this website as a directory of churches they might feel comfortable within.

The idea of a LGBT+ inclusive church is appealing to far more than just LGBT+ people, for reasons that I had never considered. Over the past five years, I've worked with dozens of pastors who lead large evangelical congregations, but desire to lead their church through the process of LGBT+ inclusion. Every time I've entered into conversations with the straight pastors seeking to move their church forward, a pattern has emerged.

First, such pastors had begun by deconstructing their own faith and worldview. The system of belief that once seemed to work so well for them began to fall apart as they read, studied, and experience real, raw life. Yet, as pastors of evangelical communities, they were afraid that if they ever expressed these doubts and this new way of seeing their faith, they would be rejected by their congregations. Typically, accompanying this deconstruction is a gradual reconstruction of their faith with a more justice-oriented, intersectional understanding of what it means to include and embrace those who have been marginalized by the church—namely, people of color, women, those with disabilities, and LGBT+ people.

As this process progressed, these pastors eventually externalized their own fear of being excluded and rejected by their congregations and often poured their energy into advocating on behalf of the LGBT+ community. Leading their church through a process of becoming LGBT+ inclusive often opened up a space in their congregations to say honestly what they believed and how they saw the world. If this process didn't happen, the pastors typically burnt out under the pressure to live inauthentic lives in front of their churches, and left the ministry and the church altogether.

This experience isn't limited to pastors. Millions of people in congregations around the world go through this process of deconstruction of their faith, and they turn to advocating for others as a way to bring themselves out of the "closet" of doubt or progressive theology.

If your community thinks that being LGBT+ inclusive is the extent of their process of becoming truly inclusive, they are missing an integral reality of inclusion. Inclusion is bigger than any one issue or marginalized group. When a church makes the move to include those who traditionally have been excluded and marginalized, more likely than not they are also signaling a broader shift in theology and practice that will make room for others who have stepped beyond the boundaries of "traditional" (and patriarchal) Christianity and are seeking a safe space to process and reconstruct their faith.

Becoming LGBT+ affirming or engaged in any other aspect of justice and equality often causes us to rethink other aspects of our theology. For, as marginalized perspectives are added to the tapestry of our faith communities, we are challenged to see things through others' eyes.

I have watched a number of communities try to be both LGBT+ inclusive and yet hold on to a rigid, traditionalist theology. No wonder so much turbulence and dissonance results! It happens whenever you rethink the foundations of your faith, whenever you try to see life from a different point of view. Like the pastors I mentioned earlier, it is understandable that many of us do this work in already inclusive communities: they are safe spaces in which to embrace different theologies or completely deconstruct and reconstruct our theological paradigm.

The call to be inclusive is a call to embrace the broad diversity of humanity. When you open the door to include one group, you are likely opening a door to many other groups as well. Celebrate that, rather than fearing it! The Christian faith is one of ongoing reformation and renewal, one that believes that the Spirit of God is living and active in the world through humans. The more diversity our communities welcome and embrace, the more we reflect the image and likeness of our multi-faceted God. But, likewise, the more diversity we welcome and embrace, the less control we will have over what people believe and how people act.

But control is not the purpose of the church. Instead, God calls us to be a community in which all of our diversity is both celebrated and de-emphasized, where we seek a unity that is deeper than skin, sexuality, gender, or religious beliefs—namely, an expansive, spiritual union with God, our world, and each other. To be truly inclusive is to welcome the messiness and splendor of human perspectives and to give up any hope of certainty or conformity. When we open the door to true inclusion, it will always lead to folks stepping out of their fear-based chambers and into the freedom of finally being able to be who they are and say what they think—and that's a beautiful reality.

Inclusive communities become safe havens for those who are leaving rigid theological communities, those who have been marginalized, and those who have never felt they fit in. They become places where a lot of broken people with a lot of work to do show up and seek to be involved and empowered. This is often the opposite of what happens in belief-restricted and exclusive communities. Walk into any evangelical megachurch and I guarantee that what you will find is a couple of thousand people with similar skin color, income level, political affiliation, and general worldview. You'll find people who are comfortable and see their church as an extension of the culture and community in which they live. Very few people will be challenged to see another perspective—and, if they are, it's so that perspective can be refuted. These sterile communities look as if they're flourishing, but they send a clear message: unless you are like us, you don't belong here.

On the flip side, communities that embrace true inclusion become places where people from all walks of life are connected, where those people come who are seeking to be empowered to do God's work of justice rather than to conform. These are people who are breaking free from the religious and social pressures that surround them and want to be more truly whole, who are dedicated to growing, and who likely have been excluded or pushed out of conformist communities—be it family, friends, or a church. They may not be interested in Sunday service or Wednesday Bible study, but love to go to your community's yoga class, meditation group, and discussion circles at a local pub. Truly inclusive communities measure their "success" not by Sunday service attendance or those who have entered into their "discipleship" process (which usually is just a process to ensure volunteer attendance and financial contributions); it is measured by people engaged throughout the week in various activities and manifestations of community that offer opportunities for healing, growth, and health.

When we embrace this "values-centered" model of community rather than a "boundary-confined" model, it becomes really hard to create traditional communities of theological or moral conformity. If your community centers itself on core values such as authenticity, peace, justice, equality, love, and wholeness, the way that individual people will manifest these attributes will look very different. At the same time, moving away from a common set of doctrines that you proclaim, or moral boundaries you profess, makes it hard for people to keep coming together in agreement. When we embrace "true inclusion," we have to rethink our entire way of doing spiritual community and life in general.

The Revolving Door

If you read any book written in the last fifty years, or take any class on pastoring and church *planting* (a word that refers to starting new churches), you'll find that one of the primary topics discussed is church growth. The focus has been on creating the biggest and most innovative congregations, which keep people throughout the entirety of their lives. This model seemed to work for about twenty years, during the rise of "megachurches" in the United States; but, by the middle of the first decade of the twenty-first century, not only megachurches, but *all* churches across the U.S. began to decline. As I noted in an early chapter, I have become convinced that the goal of a healthy spiritual community is *not* to create faithful, lifelong members. In fact, I think this goal is ultimately harmful to the individuals who are a part of the community, and that it allows abuse to flourish.

In fact, I don't believe that "keeping" people should be the goal of any church. No single community of faith can foster the kind of growth and development that is needed at every stage of an individual's life. Instead, various communities offer various tools for the stages of a person's growth or development. The church I currently pastor, Missiongathering Christian Church in San Diego, is a progressive, inclusive, quasi-evangelical church. We're a church for the postmodern deconstructionists who have left a more traditional conservative version of faith and are rethinking and rebuilding a new kind of spirituality. The folks that show up at our church are usually looking for healing from the deep wounds that religious communities have inflicted on them. I often hear newcomers say, "If it wasn't for Missiongathering, I would never go back to church." That's not a statement about how great my sermons are (as much as I would like to believe it is!) but a statement about where those folks are on their spiritual journey and what Missiongathering offers.

But the truth is that many of the people who come and find healing at Missiongathering may in fact eventually leave church all together and adopt another form of spiritual practice—such as meditation, yoga, or a more universal spirituality. Some will stop going to church, and instead choose to serve food at a homeless shelter or work in a social justice program. This is actually a measure of "success" for our church! If people find reconciliation and healing with religion and spirituality in our community, if our teaching draws them deeper into the message of Christ, that is what we want! True discipleship doesn't end in the church; it should lead people beyond the walls of the church to a deeper, richer, more integrated spirituality.

Of course, there are exceptions. Some folks will continue to attend Missiongathering for decades because they are wired for a community like this—that's great too. Others will not be interested in moving beyond the progressive Christianity we offer, and that's great too. But the goal of any inclusive community should be to welcome folks in, wherever they're at, help them find healing, integration, and wholeness, and then let them move on if that's what folks want to do. It benefits few people when a single faith community tries to become the single source of spiritual development for every person at every stage of life. This was the problem with the megachurch model, and why so many megachurches resigned themselves to being primarily for "seekers." The megachurch was a modernized evangelistic technique to connect people to Christianity, but few such churches were equipped to take people deeper into spiritual growth. Those that tried to create other programs to help folks go deeper eventually started alternative church communities within the larger church, because it's nearly impossible to help people at all levels of spiritual development in one service.

I believe inclusive churches are in fact called to have revolving doors—continually welcoming new people in to discover what it means to be a part of a faith that promotes justice, and then sending them on their way with our blessings. In this way, we prevent our community from becoming diluted by trying to offer everything to everyone, we encourage people to become the fully formed humans that God created them to be, and we continually have space and resources to help new people who are seeking a community of healing and restoration.

To help you decide what it is that your community should be like, do the hard work of asking "Who are we?" Ask: What are the distinctive factors that make our community unique? Why do people show up? What do they receive? Whatever answers emerge should be the answers that you lean into as you become inclusive. What does it look like to apply inclusivity to being a theologically rich community? What does it look like to apply inclusivity to a community with a vibrant prayer life?

In the process of becoming inclusive, it's tempting to try to become so inclusive that faith communities lose any sense of vision or identity. Instead, I encourage churches to embrace their position and their gifts, lean in to them fully, and realize that the goal is never to become a *large* faith community, but a vibrant one that actually helps improve lives and the world.

Inclusion in Context

It is one thing to talk about inclusion in abstract theological, philosophical, or political terms. It's quite another thing to be inclusive in a real, flesh-and-blood community. Perhaps it'll surprise you to know that it's actually far easier to move a community toward inclusion in reality than it is to sit back and speculate about all that might happen if we attempt to be inclusive. Most of our worst-case scenarios never take place, and if done with a robust theological underpinning, empathic understanding, and gracious patience, most communities will eagerly embrace a truly inclusive posture. Nonetheless, challenges will arise, both personally and at a communal level. To be well-equipped to face such challenges, we can lean on the wisdom of those who have already done the work of inclusion.

Even though I have had the chance to work with leaders to implement inclusivity in a number of churches around the world, and even though I now serve as a pastor of an increasingly inclusive community, I think it will benefit you if I bring in some outside perspectives at this point, perspectives of practitioners who have been engaged in the important work of inclusion for decades. So here I share with you the wisdom of practitioners who have worked for inclusion individually, in the local church, in denominations, and on a much larger scale than I do. These voices come from a wide range of backgrounds, contexts, and perspectives, but all of them share a commitment to intersectional inclusion and each has invaluable wisdom for anyone wanting to practice inclusion.

As you read through these perspectives, there will be some information that resonates, and some that doesn't. Not every answer aligns with every principle or idea that I promote in the text of this book. Nonetheless, I feel it's important to listen intently to these trusted perspectives and weigh their wisdom and experience against the realities that each of us faces.

The Voices

Jayne Ozanne is a leading gay evangelical who works to ensure full inclusion of all LGBT+ Christians at every level of the Church. She is the director of the Ozanne Foundation, a LGBT+ charity chaired by the Bishop of Liverpool in England, which works with religious organizations around the world to eliminate discrimination based on sexuality or gender. It embraces and celebrates the equality and diversity of all. Jayne was a founding member of the Church of England's Archbishops' Council, and is now back on General Synod (the Church of England's parliament) working with a growing number of allies and colleagues from other LGBT+ organizations to campaign for a more inclusive and loving Church.

Paula Williams is the president of RLT Pathways, Inc., a nonprofit organization providing counseling and coaching services in Lyons, Colorado. She is also the pastor of preaching and worship at Left Hand Community Church in Longmont, Colorado. Paula serves on the board of the Gay Christian Network, the Union of Affirming Christians, and Open Launch, a national church planting ministry. As a transgender pastor, Paula has been featured in *The New York Times*, the *Denver Post*, on *Colorado Public Radio*, in *The Huffington Post,* and on *TEDxMileHigh.*

Jonathan B. Hall is the senior pastor at First Christian Church, Colorado Springs, Colorado. He was born and raised in Huntsville, Alabama, and holds a BA in Religion and Sociology/Anthropology from Transylvania University, a MDiv from Eden Theological Seminary, a DMin in Spiritual Formation from Claremont School of Theology, and a Certificate of Ecumenical Studies from Bossey Ecumenical Institute in Geneva, Switzerland.

Michael J. Adee is a human rights advocate who has been working in the LGBT+ and HIV-AIDS communities since 1988. He earned his PhD in Communication at Louisiana State University. He has been involved in both LGBT+ political and faith-work organizing. He served as the executive director of Stonewall

Cincinnati and then as the executive director of More Light Presbyterians. He served as the chair of the founding board of the Institute for Welcoming Resources, the faith work project of the National Gay and Lesbian Task Force. He serves on a global working group associated with the International Lesbian and Gay Association (ILGA), creating the Global Interfaith Network. Michael directs the Global Faith and Justice Project of the Horizons Foundation, San Francisco.

Brian Carr is the planting and lead pastor of Missiongathering Christian Church in Issaquah, Washington. He became an ordained minister for the Christian Church (Disciples of Christ) in 2015. He previously served as a chaplain at Cincinnati Children's Hospital and has worked as a hospice chaplain in multiple retirement communities throughout Ohio. In 2017, he joined the Missiongathering Movement, a movement that starts progressive, neighborhood churches that focus on mission and social justice, and was hired to start a new church in Issaquah, Washington, where he could build an inclusive and affirming church from the ground up.

The Questions

• *What does it mean for a church to be inclusive?*

Michael Adee: We would have hoped that by "being church" and by following Christ's teachings and example, a church would automatically be inclusive, right? How I wish that [were] the case, or the case more often than not. Churches say "everyone is welcome" in their church signs, on banners displayed in front of the church, on their social media pages and websites. Pastors are often heard saying this in nearly every worship service. An inclusive church is one that...take[s] seriously the call of Christ to love God and to love their neighbors as they love themselves. And "neighbors" means anyone God brings [our] way, not just the people who look like us, believe like us, vote like us, or live next door. "Neighbor" for Jesus mean[s] anyone and everyone.

[Being a neighbor] is a high calling for any person or church. In the context of the historically white Christian denominations and traditions in the United States, the neighbor has likely been the person of color—the African American or Hispanic person—or maybe women in the more conservative traditions where women were relegated to second-class status in the church in a theological hierarchy where men ruled and men made the rules.

Across the spectrum of denominations and faith traditions of all theological positions or cultural identity, for the last fifty years the question "Is the homosexual my neighbor?" (as illustrated by Virginia Ramey Mollenkott and Letha Scanzoni in their 1978 ground-breaking eponymous book) has been the central one with regard to inclusion.

Paula Williams: An inclusive church is a congregation that does its best to understand the equality of all humans before God, and recognizes there is no individual or group not encompassed in the arms of a loving God.

Jayne Ozanne: Many churches claim to be "inclusive," when in fact they're not. They have large billboards outside that boldly state "All Are Welcome," and their congregants sincerely believe this to be true. However, the reality is that, for many of these churches, what they really mean is "all are welcome" to cross the threshold—but then there is an unspoken expectation that you will need to change various aspects of your lifestyle, identity, or ways of being before you can be made to feel fully welcome and accepted. Their welcome is conditional—it is only for "people like us," particularly if you want to be involved in any form of service in the church.

Saying a church is inclusive can therefore be quite misleading. So how do you *know* whether it is or not? I think the best way to explain inclusivity is to explain what it *feels* like to be part of an inclusive church, particularly amongst those of us who are so often excluded

First and foremost, you feel loved and fully accepted, *just as you are*. No ifs, no buts, no maybes or caveats. Unconditionally, totally loved. Whether you're standing there in a fur coat or an old pair of jeans, whether you're carrying a screaming toddler or wheeling in an old senile member of your family. Black, white, rich, poor, old, young. Just *loved*. You see, you arrive, and you immediately know you can relax, because you can see a church that is made up of an extraordinarily diverse band of brothers and sisters. There are no hidden norms, no expectations, no false smiles, and no unspoken rules. Just love.

So what *does* it mean for a church to be inclusive? I believe the answer is that unconditional love is truly in their DNA. They know that is what their vision, their mission, and their action plan is: just *love*. They put this love ahead of everything else—the need to be right, the need to be righteous, the need to be slick and professional and perfect. Of course, none of these things is wrong, it's just they should always be secondary to the primary goal of just loving.

So an inclusive church allows dyslexic, stuttering teenagers to read the lesson (if they want to); it encourages naughty children to be present and participate; it finds a way for those with poor mobility to administer communion; it embraces same-sex couples and celebrates their love; it gives past offenders a second chance and helps them build a better life; it gives a seat next to others for the unwashed, local homeless stranger; and [it] comforts the pregnant teenager crying in the back row. And it does it naturally, without thinking.

It just loves. And it leaves the rest to God.

Brian Carr: For a church to be truly inclusive, it needs to be so in both thought and in action. Oftentimes, there are churches that say they are welcoming to all, and will widely proclaim this sentiment on signs and websites and mission statements. But those same churches can also feel very unwelcoming in experience. Saying that you're inclusive is a wonderful place to start, but it is only the beginning of the process. Churches have to live out this inclusion through their leadership and through the way the church functions. If a church claims to be welcoming to the LGBTQ+ community, but then does not empower them to be leaders, never talks about sexuality and gender identity as a church, and does no outreach to that community, is that really inclusion? If a church claims to be inclusive of those who are still figuring out their faith, but then preaches a message that there is only one right path and those folks better hurry up and get on it, then is that really inclusion? The real [question] that inclusive churches need to ask themselves is: "Where does the rubber meet the road when it comes to our inclusive statements and ideas?" If they struggle to come up with...answers..., then there is a lot of work that still needs to be done.

Another way that a church can be inclusive, even if this seems counterintuitive, is, on some level, to be exclusive. What I mean when I say this is that a truly inclusive church has to exclude certain ideas and the people who profess them. An inclusive church is one where a safe space is created for people to live into or figure out who they are, and to explore and examine their spirituality. If there are ideologies and people within the church who enact violence (whether that be physical, emotional, or spiritual), then the concept of a safe space is negated. Those people will create an exclusionary environment, making certain groups of people feel unsafe and unwelcome. People who loudly proclaim racism, sexism, homophobia, and transphobia within the church can and will destroy whatever inclusive progress that church has worked toward. Now, does this mean we simply abandon the people proclaiming these viewpoints? Not necessarily. And it may be the responsibility of the pastor or other leaders to meet with those people outside of the church in an attempt to help change their hearts and minds. But if this process occurs openly within the confines of normal church functions, it will threaten to push away those who are directly threatened by those harmful ideologies. So a church that claims to stand up for, uplift, empower, and include the marginalized and outsider must also be willing to stand up to those who would use hate to spread fear, and loudly shout: "Not here!"

• *How did you come to understand the importance of being inclusive?*

Michael Adee: I grew up in a small town in southern Louisiana. Our family was deeply involved in the small Presbyterian church [there], Westminster Presbyterian Church, in a sea of Catholics and Baptists. My dad was an elder and taught the adult Sunday school class. My mom was in charge of pastoral care, making sure that every family received support in a time of need, sickness, or death. I loved going to church as a kid. I loved going to church as a teenager, and even went to the Baptist church with my friends because they had a youth group, a youth choir, and a gym where we could play basketball. When I went to college, I immediately became involved in campus ministry. I was selected to be the president of the campus ministry. I served as a student summer missionary in Africa and served as a counselor at a Christian summer camp.

Encouraged by others, I went to seminary and it was there [that] I began to struggle with my sexuality. I could not fathom the church as a safe place for me to reconcile my faith and my being gay. So I stopped going to church. The church should and can be the first place, rather than the last place, to provide safe places for everyone to discover who they are, their core values and their purpose in life, regardless of sexual orientation, gender identity, or gender expression.

Inclusion might begin with the intention to include LGBTQ people and their families, but it certainly does not stop there. Inclusion is a journey, not a destination. A church should consistently ask: "Who might not feel, or perceive that they are not, welcome here, that they do not belong here? Who might not feel or actually be safe in our church, with us?" And then the next question is: "Why? Why might they not feel welcome here, or safe with us? What is it about us, who we are, what we say, what we teach [about] the Bible, what we say about God, or how what we say or do not say about current social issues that could [cause] someone or a group of people...not [to] feel welcome or included at our church?"

More often than not, the proverbial—and the real—finger is pointed at the other, the person who is on the outside, the stranger, the ones perceived to be different, the outliers, those being excluded intentionally or not in the reality of this work of inclusion. The truth is, the finger needs to be pointed back to us, those on the inside, the church. We are the ones to be responsible, to be accountable in these faith and justice questions about who is included, who feels excluded, why this is so, and what we—the included—are going to do about this.

Paula Williams: As with most major shifts in my life, it happened in fits and starts. Back in the '90s, I hired an employee who told me when I hired him that he was gay. I said that would be fine, as long as he didn't enter into a relationship. Though I did not believe it would be wrong to enter into a same-sex relationship, I did know it would not be accepted by my denomination. Unfortunately, I thought it was important to remain within the denomination to bring about change from within. That didn't work out so well, since when I came out as transgender, the ministry I had directed for decades took a stronger stand against gay relationships than it ever had before.

I now realize I was wrong. There is no [other] way to confront injustice than to confront injustice. Lives are at stake. I will always regret not taking a stand sooner. The notion of bringing about change from within is misguided. Most real change...occurs from outside the system, not from within.

Jayne Ozanne: I recognize that homophobic prejudice exists within all streams of the Christian Church. Given [that] I was brought up as an evangelical, it was in these churches that fear and exclusion came home to me personally—though my story can be replicated in so many other places.

As it happened, I have spent most of my life going to evangelical churches that I believed were truly inclusive. I heard it in the welcome given by the pastor at the start of each Sunday service, and saw it on the welcome card placed on every chair. I didn't realize we weren't inclusive until I found myself on "the wrong side" of the "acceptable" barrier.

If I had bothered to look more closely, I'd have realized it when I was told someone was asked to stop playing in the worship band because they had entered into a same-sex relationship. More recently I've heard of friends being asked to stop doing children's ministry because they were found out to be "same-sex attracted." Others have found themselves taking off the communion rotas, prayer rotas, reading rotas as they were deemed no longer "sound," no longer fit to serve, no longer "clean"—all because of their sexual identity.

When I first came out, I tried to continue going to the evangelical church I had long been part of, [now along] with my new partner. Suddenly I found [that] people who would [normally] have greeted me with a hug shying away from me. Seats were left empty around us. People would turn and walk away from us. Nothing was said—well, not to my face—but the silence was deafening.

And then I started to see it: you needed to conform to belong. You needed to fit [this church's] idea of "normal" and "acceptable" to be able to serve and be included. I left—hurt, upset, and heartbroken. No one followed up or asked me why I no longer [came]. It took some time for me to risk crossing the threshold of another church again. The risk of rejection was just too great, and my pain was just too raw.

As it happened, I was wooed back to church by my local Anglican vicar, who ran the parish church just across the road from where I lived. I'd been once or twice before, but its Anglo-Catholic/traditional style wasn't what I'd been used to, and the people were, well, different.

I live in a very poor part of Oxford, with very high deprivation levels—we tick every box: drug and alcohol abuse, pensioner poverty, single mothers, mental health problems. I'm fortunate: I live in one of the old village houses, which is over five hundred years old. I'm seen as one of the "posh" ones—the lady in the big house. Never mind that I live by faith, I'm seen as rich. I've had a good education, I drive a car, and I have hope of a better future. It was *I* who was different, I realized—and not because of my sexuality.

But that first Sunday I was greeted with more love and warmth than anywhere else I have ever been. During our short service, I looked around and saw such a wide variety of people, none of whom would have gone anywhere near the "successful city center church." In many ways I'm glad they hadn't, as...they would have felt completely out of place if they had.

At the end of the service, the elderly lady in the pew in front turned around to greet me. She had recognized me from my participation in the Christmas Carol Service the year before, when I had been asked to help out at the last minute by playing my violin in the music group. "So lovely to see you again, Jayne. Is this your partner? Can I meet her?" She must have seen the look of confusion on my face, as I struggled to know what to say for the best. Taking my hand, she gently said, "It's alright dear, my husband became a woman just before he died. You know, we're *all very* welcome here!" I couldn't work out whether to laugh or cry. But I did know I was unquestionably welcomed, loved, and accepted, as was my partner. This was a truly inclusive church—and we had come home.

• **Was there a time when you embraced a theology or worldview of exclusion? What was the impetus of that perspective?**

Michael Adee: I grew up in a racist, sexist, homophobic, and heterosexist society and culture in south Louisiana in the 1960s and '70s. So this was the era I grew up in, sadly, so how could it not have affected me directly or indirectly in terms of the development of my faith, theology, view of myself, my understanding of what it meant to be the church? A question for the church striving to be inclusive: how does it recognize and address its own collective, systemic, historic heterosexism and homophobia, sexism and racism? Surely these persistent and pervasive, sometimes silent, sometimes vocal elements need to be addressed in the journey to inclusion.

Jayne Ozanne: I'm not sure I would say I ever consciously embraced a theology of exclusion—I, like those around me, believed in the unconditional love of God for all. The truth is, however, I lived, without knowing it, in a very small bubble—and my theology had never really been tested. I worshiped at a church that was populated with people "just like me." As all sociologists will tell you, like attracts like, and so, without even meaning to, we became monochrome.

It is interesting to note that I don't remember ever hearing [a single] sermon on the subject of homosexuality. The sinfulness of being actively gay was just something we all *knew* to be true. The Bible was "clear" on it, spelled out in six verses. More importantly, it was something we just "knew in our spirits"; this internal "witness of truth" is what counted most. It was wrong and sinful; people just needed to repent and be healed, or live a celibate life. Easy theology to have in your head; more difficult when faced with the reality of a gay couple standing right in front of you. But, of course, we never were. They never came, we never encountered, and so we just carried on in our bubble, oblivious to the pain we caused.

I don't think any of us meant to be homophobic—we would have denied it vigorously if you [had] told us we were. But sadly, unwittingly even, this was the reality. We were so stuck in our monochrome little bubble, we had no idea of the multicolored life outside our nest.

Jonathan Hall: I grew up in the Bible Belt. I remember hearing ministers from my friends' churches speaking negatively about inclusion. Even at a young age, these destructive statements went against all that I knew about faith and the Bible. At that time, I was not a completely inclusive person, but I was beginning the journey towards inclusion.

For me, like with many others, it was knowing someone who was excluded and bashed because of their sexuality that opened my eyes. At some point, our understanding of the Bible, tradition, reason, and experience do not align as neatly as they once did. I am thankful to have been a part of spiritual community (even though it was in the Bible Belt), that made room for all of us at the table.

Brian Carr: For the majority of my life I embraced both a theology and worldview of exclusion. I grew up in a conservative, rural area of Ohio where diversity did not really exist, nor was it ever a topic of conversation. I was surrounded by bigotry and ignorance for the first eighteen years of my life and admittedly did nothing to combat it. My interactions were with white, straight (I assumed), conservative Christians, and anyone who did not fit that archetype was somehow considered "wrong." I did not put much thought into why they were wrong, or how exactly they were wrong, but I just knew it deep down. I had the privilege of never needing to challenge those assumptions, and so I did not.

I also grew up going to a fairly conservative church, one whose theological foundation was built on sin and hell as things of utmost concern. This meant that anything that was sinful and went against God was another brick laid on the path to hell. I believed what I was taught by my pastors and Sunday school teachers, because who was I to challenge their authority? One of the sins we were lectured on was homosexuality, and how evil it was. I bought into this idea and regularly used "gay" as an insult and called those I didn't like "fags." If I didn't like you, I could paint you as a homosexual who was sinning and walking the path straight to hell—a fair punishment in my mind for annoying me during my youth.

This worldview began to change as I moved away from my conservative cocoon and began interacting with more progressive-minded people, people of color, women who weren't quiet and submissive, and people who openly identified as LGBTQ+. I am grateful to this day that there were people willing to be patient with me as I worked through my own bigotry and prejudicial viewpoints as I started my journey toward peeling back the layers of my own racism, misogyny, and homophobia. The result of this is a greater awareness of the privilege, racism, misogyny, and homophobia that I still have in me and how to continually combat it. I also learned that one of the greatest ways I can be an ally to the groups I...actively [used] to exclude is to have the same patience with those currently living exclusive lives as people showed me. It's imperative that we don't simply give up on them, but continue to work in ways that can move them forward into the inclusive world we hope to build.

• What is the biggest barrier to inclusion?

Michael Adee: I believe and have experienced a number of the most significant barriers to inclusion. A key one is this: "But we are already inclusive!" which is either innocent, or malevolent. Another barrier is fear in terms of: "What will the church become if we include those people?"—whoever *those* people happen to be. A[nother] barrier is the preponderance of conflict avoiders within the church, which might be the pastors, church leadership, or particular church members who are invested in maintaining the status quo.

If there is a history of fundamentalist teaching of the Bible that denigrates women, LGBTQ people, or people of color, then such teaching and the attitudes encouraged or sanctioned by them of sexism, homophobia, and racism are barriers to inclusion. A final barrier is related to responsibility and accountability if the already-there, included people hold the opinion or belief that those who have been historically excluded are to do the work of inclusion so that they earn their place in the church, in the pew, at the communion table, or in the pulpit.

Paula Williams: I believe the biggest barrier to inclusion is money. Many large church evangelical pastors do not believe a monogamous relationship with a person of the same sex is a sin. I also know their largest givers believe it is a sin, and these men (for they are all men) are not willing to go up against those givers. As one megachurch pastor said to me five years ago, "I know the culture has moved on, but my money hasn't."

The second-biggest barrier is power. Church leaders who lead their congregations toward inclusion lose status. Most are not willing to pay that price.

Jonathan Hall: In my experience, the biggest barrier to inclusion that I hear in my community is that: "If we become an Open and Affirming congregation, we are somehow losing our identity." I have heard it explained as [that we would be] losing our history and our values even though we are proposing [only that we state] clearly what we ha[ve] been living out for decades. This type of reservation can be embodied in a variety of ways.

My answer is always the same: We are not changing who we are or who we have been. We are, actually, becoming more of who we have always been. We are not changing our values; instead, we are being clear about our values, hopes, and dreams for the world because of the One who made us all.

Brian Carr: I think the two biggest barriers to inclusion are power and fear. Power is an intoxicating drug and one that we are taught to take as often as possible. Part of the "American Dream," at its core, is collecting and wielding power—whether that be through money, influence, or status. In order to have power, there must be those among us who have little to no power. It's the only way it can work. If everyone had power, then would anyone really have power? The answer, in its simplest terms, is no. An aggregation of power at the top (by people, corporations, or governments) requires that there be people at the bottom who are at the mercy of their power.

I highlight this to say that if a person or group of people wants to accumulate power, then they need to ensure that another person or group of people doesn't have power. For white people to maintain power, there need to be people of color without power. For men to maintain power, there need to be women without power. For Christianity to maintain power, there have to be other religious groups without power. And this is where the barrier to inclusion comes in.

Inclusion means a sharing of power among all people within that community. A truly inclusive church cannot have one group that is more powerful than other groups. If a church gives more power, whether implicitly or explicitly, to white members, then it cannot be a church that is truly inclusive to people of color. If you have people within the church who are grasping [on]to their power (even if it's power that can only be wielded within the church) then they will be resistant to true inclusion because they do not wish to decentralize the power they have. As pastors, we have to reframe what power looks like, reflecting the biblical wisdom that power is actually weakness and will not hold up within the "kindom" of God. Jesus did not come to grasp and centralize power, but rather to humble those with power and uplift those without. He came to set all things equal—a call we must follow.

Another barrier to inclusion is fear: fear of the unknown, fear of differences, fear of uncertainty. Fear of losing the above-mentioned power plays a role as well. But I am also talking about fearing the stranger. We as humans tend to insulate ourselves with people who look, think, and act similarly to us. There are benefits to this type of community building, but also a host of problems as well. When we surround ourselves solely with "like people," we can begin to fear those who are different from us. This type of insulation creates ignorance about other groups of people, and ignorance is a precursor to fear. We often fear that which we do not know.

This issue doesn't just occur in parts of America that are fairly monolithic (such as rural Ohio, where I grew up), but can also occur in the most diverse of cities. New York City, Los Angeles, and Seattle are home to plenty of people who prefer exclusion over inclusion. This fear can be another barrier to people struggling to move toward inclusion. Humans are very good at taking differences they find in other people and turning them into threats rather than learning experiences. Again, we as pastors have the responsibility of creating churches that show the beauty of diversity, and of highlighting the fact that people who are different from us are still created in the image of God.

• *If a church community decided it wanted to become more inclusive, what advice would you give to them?*

Michael Adee: The first question I would ask a church community that decided it wanted to become more inclusive is: "Why?" This might seem like a cavalier or unkind question, [but] the truth is that the motivations will surface during the process or be sensed those who are being "included" anyway, so it is helpful for all concerned to have a clear understanding of what is driving the move toward inclusion.

The advice I would offer is: make sure that you, the church, do the inside work first of addressing any of the barriers to inclusion before inviting people to join you. The work of addressing racism is not to be done "on" the people of color, the work of ending sexism is not to be done "on" women, and the work of challenging homophobia is not to be done "on" the LGBTQ people and their families.

The process of inclusion is as important as the goal of inclusion. Church people are human beings; we have differing feelings, beliefs, values, and life experiences. A process that creates safe and generous space for all of these human elements of a church to surface, be validated even if not agreed with, or condoned, allows for everyone to be part of the process. Some people will absent themselves by not participating in the open forums, the small group sessions, the Bible studies. No one can be forced into inclusion—the process or the state. It is a journey. When people withdraw, this is the time for the intervention of a private one-to-one conversation wherein a pastor or church [leader] requests such a confidential visit. It is in this kind of setting that a person may indeed feel safe[r] to speak their mind, share their fears, ask their questions. And, certainly, they can experience validation by an intentional visit by a pastor or other church leader.

Paula Williams: I would suggest they talk with other churches that have recently been through the process. I believe [that] the experience[s] of Forefront Church in Brooklyn, New York; Denver Community Church in Denver; NewStory Church in Chicago; and Eastlake Church in Seattle, [have prepared them to] have excellent advice to give to those who are just beginning to consider the costs and benefits of becoming open and affirming.

• Is there a cost to becoming inclusive?

Paula Williams: Using traditional metrics, it looks like most evangelical churches that become inclusive lose about 10 percent of their people and 20 percent of their money. (Conservative people do tend to give more.) Disappointingly, a lot of the[se churches] have also discovered that they lose most of their people of color. The reasons for that are not clear, though it may be because the denominations in America most often associated with people of color are also more conservative denominations.

Jayne Ozanne: There is always a cost to doing anything worthwhile. St. Ignatius of Loyola recognized this, and summed it up perfectly in a prayer that calls us to: *"Give and not to count the cost...to labor and not ask for any reward, save that of knowing that we do thy will."*

I believe that there are three major costs which I personally have become aware of.

The first and most obvious is to our pride—specifically, admitting that we have been wrong. I now personally realize that the "witness" I had felt in my spirit, which I so firmly believed to be the voice of the Holy Spirit, was in fact the "witness" of a "homophobic spirit." I say this purposefully, knowing it may well shock many, but it is the truth as I have experienced it. You see, it was only when I confronted and repented of my own internalized homophobia—some years after my coming out—that I finally found the peace that silenced all the incessant voices arguing around in my head. I had unwittingly and unknowingly imbibed a homophobic narrative from youth, which I needed to recognize and repent of to find peace.

I would implore you that if you [likewise] truly believe that the Holy Spirit has told you "same-sex love is wrong," please do look again at what has formed this. Have you truly searched the Scriptures, or have you just grown up with a cultural norm that you believed to be true? It requires great humility and grace to admit we are wrong, but God is more than willing and able to forgive us. It is the Way of the Cross—with repentance and forgiveness at its core, but rest assured we never walk it alone.

The second cost can wound us deeply, as it is a cost to our reputation and our standing within our community, church, and friends. When I came out, I sadly lost the vast majority of my friends, and it caused great difficulties within my immediate family. Some, over time, have reassessed their own views—challenged by the witness of the fruit they could see blossoming in my life as I finally came to know the joy and peace of what it was to love and be loved. Others have distanced themselves from me, unsure of what to say and preferring silence over dialogue.

Our aim should never be to be popular, but to do what we truly believe is right and stand up for what we believe God is calling us to.

The third cost is arguably the hardest and the most difficult to bear. It is to be constantly ridiculed, misunderstood, and scorned by those we used to know as friends. It is to have our faith questioned and our integrity impugned. We are told that we are pandering to the social norms of the day, going soft on the importance of scripture, and exchanging the truth of God for a lie.

No matter what they say, though, we must come in the opposite spirit—choosing to "just *love*."

Christ himself tells us (Luke 6:27–28): *"Love your enemies, do good to those who hate you, bless those who curse you, pray for those who mistreat you"*[NIV]. And that is hard. But it is the "Way of Love"—which is the Way of the Cross, and rest assured we never walk it alone. Never.

Jonathan Hall: I think that it is easy to be fearful of what the costs may be to be inclusive. We may lose people in our churches because they think that we have lost God. For me, when we move towards inclusion, we are not worshiping exclusivity and close-mindedness. Additionally, we are not associating the Divine with exclusion. Thankfully, we are not alone on this journey. We are following in the footsteps of our spiritual ancestors who were first called atheists in the Roman Empire. They were called atheists because they did not deify [the] exclusivity and close-mindedness found within the Roman Imperial cult. They refused to deify things that were not God and actions that were not associated with their experiences with Jesus Christ. Perhaps it is time for us to stop deifying things that are not God. In other words, if there is a cost to becoming inclusive, then it entails walking away from our spiritual communities, friends, families, etc.—just as our spiritual ancestors did—those that deify things that are not God.

Brian Carr: I think there is a cost to being inclusive, though [it is] different for every person or community that moves toward inclusion. One of the individual costs to being inclusive is the potential loss of family or friends who disagree with the type of people you are trying include. Toxic relationships can form when you are friends with someone who believes homosexuality is a sin while you are trying to be inclusive to the LGBTQ+ community. Family relationships can break down when your father makes racist comments about people you love. Work can become hostile when you confront a coworker about the sexist joke they made in the break room. There can be a personal human cost to your inclusion, but by welcoming more communities and people into your life, you are opening...doors to deeper and more fulfilling relationships that can replace the ones you might have lost.

There can also be the personal cost of losing power or attention or popularity. As a straight, white, cis-male, I have had power and been at the center of every conversation my entire life. Part of the move toward inclusion means moving farther away from the center yourself so that there is room for more voices in the conversation. People like me are born in the center and have the option to fight tooth and nail to stay there. But the simple move of stepping out toward the margins can have an important impact on yourself and your community. Now, is this a devastating loss to me? No. But it is a loss nonetheless and can often be a deterrent for some people as they wonder how inclusive they should try to be. However, the benefit to the community as a result of whatever loss you may incur as an individual always makes this a worthwhile tradeoff.

Communities can also suffer losses when becoming more inclusive, and churches offer firsthand experience of this. If a church moves to become open and affirming toward the LGBTQ+ community, you will undoubtedly lose members of your church who disagree with such a move. And with them goes their money and time and resources, which can have a huge negative impact on a struggling church. The same goes for a church [that] wants to embrace movements like Black Lives Matter or the Women's March. I have seen churches crumble and fall apart after making these moves toward inclusion because they lose too many members or too much money.

These challenges can make inclusion seem, at times, like a death sentence. But what is worse—a church remaining financially stable but excluding those who Jesus challenges us to welcome, or a church that follows Jesus at the cost of power and money? For me, it is not even close. We are called to follow Jesus, not church attendance numbers and budgets. There is no cost too great that should stop a church from including and affirming people—people who were created in the image of God. I would rather fail as an inclusive church than thrive as an exclusive one. Plain and simple.

• **How do intersectionality and inclusivity interact, in your opinion?**

Michael Adee: Intersectionality is a reference to the reality that social justice issues are not separate, they are connected, even though our tendency or history has been to keep them separate. For example, the persistent existence of poverty in a country with historic levels of wealth must be looked at through the lenses of racism, greed on the part of too many of those with wealth, capitalism that makes people into commodities, the mass incarceration of black and brown people, and a prosperity gospel that ignores the poor or blames them for their circumstances.

Interconnectivity speaks to the divine connections across all of humanity and creation. Not only are our souls connected in some mysterious and powerful way, our fates are linked together. And our existence and survival are connected to creation and how we take care of the planet and all living things upon it.

• *Why would you encourage someone or a community to seek to embrace inclusion?*

Michael Adee: There is a liberation available to everyone in a church, youth group, or campus ministry when a commitment to inclusion is made. I believe God's Spirit is allowed more room to move in open hearts, minds, and spirits. I believe the teachings of Christ and the example of his life become more authentic within churches that seek to be inclusive and keep taking their next steps in the inclusion journey.

I also believe that God's love is reflected more clearly and in much more compelling ways from a church seeking to be inclusive, seeking to remove barriers to God's love and grace for all. If a church is committed to evangelism, then how [can] it not also be committed to inclusion? Surely inclusion and evangelism go hand in hand.

Brian Carr: I would encourage all people and communities to seek and embrace inclusion because that is the way we are meant to live. Over and over Jesus invites us to welcome and include whoever we consider as the marginalized or outsider. Over and over Jesus spends his time with those [who] society had cast out. Are we really [to] think that we can decide who's in and who's out? Especially when Jesus was willing continually [to] cross the boundaries that society had set up to exclude people?

We are meant to live in inclusive and diverse communities, to truly become one body. This doesn't mean that we water down each other's cultures until we all look, think, and act the same. A body is not made up entirely of hands or of knees. It is made up of radically different parts that create a whole. Similarly, we are called to celebrate the diversity of those around us and create a community out of this diversity, even if it's not always perfect in the way that we understand perfection.

It is my sincerest belief that God created humans to live in community with one another, and [that] we can't have true community until we include those who are different from us. An inclusive community gives so much life to each individual, and can create wholeness out of brokenness. I have participated in many churches and I've found that I always leave exclusive churches with less than what I came with, and always leave inclusive churches with more. That is reason enough for me to continually embrace and uplift inclusion.

• • •

These voices represent a sampling of authentic practitioners of inclusion in their respective communities. What you can see is that the perspectives vary based on context, experience, and culture, but the heart of the message in all of these voices is the same: inclusion is the burning core of the gospel, and the imperative for every follower of Christ.

Conclusion

I looked and saw a huge crowd of people, which no one could even begin to count, representing every nation and tribe, people and language, standing before the throne and before the Lamb, wearing white robes and waving palm branches.
—Revelation 7:9 (VOICE)

In the beginning of the Hebrew Bible, we are told a story about how the Spirit of God created all of humanity out of one single person. Throughout the rest of the biblical narrative, we see many multiply from that one, and the diversity, complexity, and beauty of humanity increase in every corner of the earth and beyond. By the time we arrive at the apocalyptic vision of the book of Revelation, we see what is supposed to be the pinnacle of history: the gathering of people from *"every nation and tribe, people and language"* standing before the throne of the Christ in worship. We see the trajectory beginning in a state of darkness, within which God must create sources of light to shine in the universe, to a declaration of Jesus that all of humanity is "the light of the world," and, ultimately, in this same scene in the book of Revelation, where sun and flame are no longer needed, for the light of Christ enlightens every corner of the cosmos.

In these images, we see the story of gradual awakening, of redemption progressing slowly, like a seed planted in a field that finally culminates in a feast around a table, where the full diversity of humanity stands equal before the throne of God, enlivened and enlightened, living in the authentic glory of our True Selves, signified by white robes. In this picture, God's redemptive purposes have come to their completion, and the universe is as it was intended to be. In our diversity, God's divine light is magnified, and, out of many, we become yet again one. As followers of Jesus, this is the reality for which we long for and strive. A world united in its diversity, a world where all are celebrated and included, a world where discrimination and exclusion no longer have a place.

This is the culmination of the gospel and the great aim of everyone who claims to be a follower of Jesus. This should also be the aim of every single one of our churches, communities, and of our individual lives. As we come to the end of this exploration of what it means to be truly inclusive, it is my hope and prayer that we will all be challenged, convicted, and inspired by the vision given to us not only here in the book of Revelation, but throughout the entire trajectory of Scripture. To be inclusive isn't optional for followers of Christ, and it truly is the only posture that will create the peace and reconciliation that our world needs in our present day.

As I write these words, the United States is just finishing the first year of the Presidency of Donald Trump. Throughout this year, we have seen an uprising of bigotry and xenophobia in forms that many of us who live in a state of privilege believed had been dealt with in the 1960s. We have seen neo-Nazis and white supremacists rally by the hundreds in the streets; we've seen the President of the United States justify and endorse the behaviors of bigots and bona fide hatemongers; and we've seen the political polarization in the nation and indeed the world grow in intensity. It is easy to look at the state of the world in 2018 and wonder whether the inclusive gospel of Jesus has failed. I must admit I have considered this proposition more than once. But I believe the more likely reality is that we are seeing what L. Robert Keck called "the supernova effect."[1]

The term "supernova" refers to the experience of a star burning at its brightest right before it dies. In our day, we're seeing white supremacy's, homophobia's, and misogyny's last stand. I believe that we have developed all of the resources we need to deal with our deepest prejudice and begin moving our nation and world toward an inclusive posture. But, of course, it begins on the individual level. It begins with each of us confronting our participation in patriarchy. It begins with each of us committing to practice our capacity to empathize with our "others." It begins with us being willing to step beyond our comfort zone and challenge the status quo of "orthodoxy." It begins with us

---

1   L. Robert Keck, "Sacred Quest: The Evolution and Future of the Human Soul," *Sacred Quest: The Evolution and Future of the Human Soul* (New York: Chrysalis Books, 2000), 163.

recommitting ourselves to the radically subversive gospel of Jesus Christ and allowing its potency to reform and transform our lives, our churches, our communities, and our world.

Almost every Sunday, I have the unique privilege of presiding over communion at the church I pastor. Every Sunday, I find such a profound sense of joy as I see people of every race, gender identity, sexual orientation, political affiliation, and socioeconomic status gathered into our strange, rag-tag community of individuals committed to living out the words of Jesus. And every Sunday, I get to pronounce the following words as I approach the altar during our communion liturgy:

> At Missiongathering, we believe in an open table, because this table isn't our table but God's table, and God has invited every single one of us to come. No matter who you are, what you believe, where you've been, or where you will go, you are invited to come and feast on the grace and love of God, and be called to commit your life to the rhythm of Christ, who broke open his body, and poured out his life to redeem the world. You are loved, you are worthy, and you are invited to come just as you are and receive these symbols of our grace and unity in God.

When I say these words, I feel their power. They're especially powerful for me because I have sat in many church contexts that have built strong and high walls around the communion table, reserving it only for those who believed the "right things," acted the "right way," looked the "right way," or belonged to the "right group" of people. There was a time where I basked in the egoic glory of believing that I was one of the "elect" and that this table was an *exclusive* one for me and those like me. There was I time when I relished a theology of exclusion—until it became used against me. There is nothing more powerful, after experiencing the full weight of exclusion, to be invited, just as you are, with all of the "wrong" people, to come and take hold of the very body and blood of Christ.

There's something transcendent about participating in the very ritual that millions use to embody and symbolize the exclusivity of their gospel. There's something truly humbling when those whom the privileged and powerful consider "unclean" are the ones who get to serve the most sacred of elements to one another. In this sense, communion becomes an act of resistance. It becomes an embodied declaration to the powers that be that their orthodoxies and boundaries are mere illusions, and a sure sign that the kingdom of God is expanding beyond their control, that the last do indeed become first, and the unclean are declared holy.

There is something profound when all of us step boldly into our place at the table of God's grace on equal ground, fully celebrating and embracing our diversity, and rejoicing in our unity through the Spirit of Christ. The theatrics of the communion liturgy are but a shadow of the image that we find in the book of Revelation, a glimpse of the point to which God desires humanity to progress. For, we not only all stand together around the throne of the Lamb as one, but the culmination of John's vision is when each and every one of us is called to the banquet table of God.

This heavenly "marriage supper" is the ultimate metaphor for the unity that God desires through the gospel of Inclusion. For, in Christ, the many become one. One new humanity emerges as the power of the self-sacrificial love of Christ on the cross destroys the walls of division. One body emerges out of the many parts, and humanity at last lives into the truth that we are all already one. Unity and union are our fundamental nature, but we have failed to see this reality clearly. Instead of seeing what unites us, instead of celebrating the unique differences that emerge out of such unity, we have focused on our distinctives as a reason to separate and segregate. But the days of such divisiveness in our world are limited as more and more of us awaken to the inclusion imperative, and begin to do the inner and outer work of tearing down our walls and fearlessly opening wide the gates of our hearts, our churches, and the Kingdom to absolutely everyone.

This is the hope, prayer, and goal of this book—that your own passion and desire for inclusivity will be enlarged, and that you will take the steps necessary to confront your own inner prejudice and lean into the flow of the Spirit of God, which calls all of us forward toward greater love and greater inclusion. The journey of inclusion will not happen overnight, and it will inevitably throw us and our communities into periods of pain and tribulation. But as James writes so poignantly, "The testing of your faith produces endurance, and when endurance is fully developed, you will be made complete and will lack nothing" (Jas. 1:3-4). So lean in to the challenge, embrace the process, and pour out your life to build a more inclusive world. This is the work that we're called to do, the goal of our faith, and the hope of the world: that all will be welcomed to the table as equal and vital participants, bearing the full glory of God in the midst of our expansive diversity.

Appendix 1

Making True Inclusion Real in Your Context:
10 Suggested Actions

So many communities and individuals desire to embrace the gospel's call to become truly inclusive, but often that desire never materializes into anything more than conversations and aspirations. The reason for this is that most people are paralyzed by the thought of where to start. How does an individual or a community begin to practically incarnate true inclusion into their day-to-day life and ministry? The purpose of this appendix is to give some practical pointers that I have learned and witnessed in my own work as a pastor and a consultant to churches. I hope that these ideas help inspire you and your community to take the first step towards incorporating true inclusion into the fundamental DNA of your life.

---

1. Participate in regular community self-assessments and create an inclusion task force.

One of the most helpful and transformative processes that I have ever witnessed a church undertake on their journey toward embracing radical inclusivity is to establish a team of people whose job it is to analyze the congregation's inclusivity using raw data, anonymous interviews, and detailed analysis of the ways that systemic exclusion is at work in a congregation. This process either looks like hiring an external team of diversity and inclusion experts to come in and conduct an analysis of the church (which can be costly, but is worth it!) or else using a number of assessments that have been developed by various denominations and groups, such as the United Church of Christ and The Center of Assessment and Policy Development. While most official surveys focus on one primary topic (i.e., racial justice, gender equality) they can easily be adapted to pertain to intersectional inclusion as described in this book.

The process of assessing a church's current state of inclusivity can be a painful process for those who are committed to the community. Inevitably what will be revealed are large areas where a community is not excelling in inclusion and in fact, probably perpetuating exclusion. But as the community engages honestly in self-assessment, these revelations should not be seen as condemnations but motivation to continue to work to intentionally dismantle systems of oppression and exclusion at work in the community. It is essential for the community to name the areas where exclusion persists, to disclose this information to the members of the community, and create a task force that covenants to work with the church in tangible ways to overcome exclusivity and marginalization in their midst.

2. Give the voiceless back their voice.

One of the major failures of many progressive communities and individuals is what could be called the "over-zealous ally." So often, well-intentioned individuals become infuriated by injustice in their community and society and immediately begin to passionately speak up "on behalf" of marginalized communities. In some situations, speaking up on a marginalized community's behalf is essential, especially in spaces where such communities do not have the access to power or the ability to speak. But in most situations, good allyship doesn't mean speaking on a community's behalf, but rather, finding ways to uplift the voices and stories of those facing exclusion or oppression.

. What this means is using the platform of the church community, connections, and resources to amplify the voices of those who have been directly impacted by exclusive policies and procedures. In most cases, marginalized people who are seen as "silent" have actually been speaking for decades, but their voices have been silenced by the noise of the oppressor. To embrace true justice, equality, and inclusion requires that those with privilege and power use that to uplift the voices of the marginalized, allowing them to speak for themselves, tell their own stories, and demand their own justice.

How can your community begin to platform the voices and perspective of the so-called "voiceless" in your midst? Perhaps you invite activists and organizations engaged in justice work into your community's space to share their perspectives. Perhaps you hold listening groups, where the leadership team of your church sits and simply hears the experiences and perspectives of minorities in your community. Whatever you decide, be mindful of making sure that your actions and activism provide a platform for those you seek to advocate on behalf of whenever possible.

3. Do your own research.

Communities often will turn to the marginalized in their midst and request that they educate the community about their experience and perspective. After taking an assessment of your community and listening to the voices of the marginalized, it's important to remember that "the excluded" do not owe you or your community anything. No one is required to speak about their experience or their story, and the decision to not engage is not "unhelpful" but actually an essential part of many peoples own self-care. It's incredibly exhausting to continue reliving the trauma of exclusion by retelling stories over and over again.

An enormous body of literature is available to us today that deals with the experience and perspective of nearly every oppressed and marginalized group. A simple Google search or visit to your local library, civil rights center, or LGBT+ center will be able to provide you with rich and diverse resources.

Do the research yourself. Read about the history and experience of oppressed groups, and never expect or guilt a person into educating you about their experience of exclusion and oppression.

4. Never build a platform on your advocacy for others.

Far too many communities and individual allies will seek to build a brand and platform off of their advocacy and embrace of true inclusion. This is especially a temptation for communities whose activism has cost them members and money. But your allyship isn't a new project or brand for you to market and benefit from, but a raw requirement of what it means to be a follower of Jesus. Seeking to build a platform on your advocacy of the rights of others is, quite simply, a tool that perpetuates oppression. Far too many inclusive straight, white, cisgender, male pastors and leaders have secured book deals, speaking tours, and founded nonprofits on their "allyship" of marginalized communities.

In the past, this was sometimes helpful, especially when certain minorities had no hope of having their voices heard by those in power. But today, through the power of social media and the Internet, almost everyone has the ability to speak on their own behalf and be seen and heard by those with power. Therefore the role of the ally is to help the marginalized build a platform, not build a platform on the backs of their stories and experiences. Being an ally will cost you, but it has cost the marginalized infinitely more, and any attempt to profit for doing the right thing is a grievous violation of trust and calls into question the intention of the individual, leader, or community.

5. Show up to serve.

To be committed to intersectional justice requires that communities of privilege show up as servants and support to movements demanding justice for marginalized people. So often we're used to our communities and leaders being recognized and taking leadership roles in the ministries we engage in. But to be a community that is effective in the pursuit of true inclusion and justice means that we must adopt the attitude that was in Christ, "who came not to be served but to serve, and to give his life a ransom for many (Mk. 1:31)."

Truly inclusive communities must be consistent in their commitment to showing up in various venues as advocates for and supporters of marginalized people's rights. Whether these are regular protests and demonstrations such as The Women's March or Pride Parades or showing up at your statehouse when important legislation is being debated, truly inclusive communities must be engaged in robust and regular servant activism. If you're not willing to put in the work to serve your neighbor of a different race, gender identity, or sexual orientation, then you are not willing to be a truly inclusive community.

6. Intentionally deconstruct patriarchy and reconstruct with inclusivity.

Take a hard look at the leadership structure in your community—does it consist of primarily privileged and powerful classes of people? Are all sectors' voices represented and empowered? If your community is a church, does the congregation see people of different colors, sexual orientations, and genders represented on the platform? Do women hold the same kind of influence as men? Are differently-abled people or neuro-divergent individuals afforded the same leadership opportunities as everyone else?

If not, then you must intentionally begin to request that those with the most privilege and power relinquish their roles in order to uplift and provide others with positions of influence. This often feels threatening and "unfair" to those who feel that they have worked hard and earned their place in leadership. But unless the "mountains are laid low and the valley exalted," unless our privilege is nailed to the cross and we embrace the servant-leadership of Christ, we will never see Christ's radical inclusion spread through our community like we claim to desire. Until our power and leadership structures begin to reflect the world that we desire to live in, change will not be effectively manifest in the community.

7. Put your money where your activism is.

Progressive churches are often averse to the language of "missionaries," primarily because "missions" has been used as a tool of colonization and oppression by Christians for thousands of years. But perhaps it's time that our communities reclaim "mission work" by financially supporting local activists and organizations who are engaged in true Kingdom work by speaking up, acting up, and showing up to create a more just and equal world for us all. Far too many communities and individuals pay lip service to activists and their causes, but what almost every activist and organization needs is consistent financial support.

If you or your church is truly concerned about activism and justice, make a commitment to a small group of organizations and activists to financially support their work and witness in the world. In this way you are extending your ministry to places that you would never otherwise be able to reach, and doing it in a more effective and impactful way through supporting experts.

8. Repent often and publicly.

Those of us with societal privilege benefit from the oppression of the marginalized, whether or not we like it. Therefore communities that are led and dominated by privileged voices must be quick to own their privilege and the ways that it rears its ugly head of oppression in the life of the community. Leaders must be willing to repent whenever their church, denomination, or fellow ministers of the gospel embody exclusion, and do so not only with lip service, but tangible action and effort to right the wrongs done either by themselves or on their behalf by their colleagues, churches, or affiliated organizations. Only when a sincere spirit of humility and repentance is embodied will trust be established that paves the way for true justice and inclusion to be established.

As I discussed earlier in the book, repentance actually most accurately means "expand your mind." I also want to suggest that our communities be committed to listening, learning, and changing our perspectives and practice often as well—and give reasons for why the change is occurring. If the leadership team has collectively come to understand that it has embodied latent white supremacy, say that, own it, and change it in view of the public. This is the sort of faithful witness the world has not usually seen from the Church, and it's the capital that builds pathways of trust with the marginalized communities we seek to embrace.

9. Don't be a community of "response" but of consistent advocacy.

It is popular among progressive communities of faith to respond to current events and cultural moments, and to hear progressive preachers tweeting things like "If your pastor isn't speaking on XYZ tomorrow morning, maybe it's time to leave your church." While the sentiment is right—our communities should certainly be speaking boldly against injustice in our culture and society—this shouldn't be something that we do in response to tragedies or horrendous situations, but on a regular basis.

The message of radical justice and true inclusion should be in the heart of everything your community teaches and engages in, for it was at the heart of the life and ministry of Jesus. One cannot read the teachings of Jesus and not be compelled to offer consistent social critique and calls for more justice and more peace on a weekly basis. Our communities should always be proactive in our identifying of injustice and outlining constructive paths for the establishment of justice and equity. Our advocacy should be 365 days a year, not just when some event catches the attention of the national media.

---

10. Engage in regular community-wide studies, trainings, and discussions.

Most people don't realize the tremendous wealth of resources that surround them. Believe it or not, dozens of organizations in your community offer trainings, studies, and discussions on the justice matters that most affect those who live around you. Groups such as Interfaith Alliance, the American Civil Liberties Union (ACLU), the local LGBT+ Center, Faith in Action (formerly PICO), or Human Rights Campaign (HRC) are examples of collectives of justice and action that are eager to engage you and your community in conversations and trainings about the issues that matter most in your region.

Be intentional about building relationships with these local justice organizations, engaging with the leaders, sending volunteers to serve, and using the wealth of resources that are likely available to you to educate, equip, and empower your community to live into Christ's call to be truly inclusive every year.

These are just ten potential action steps your community can take to begin embracing true inclusion. All these steps require humility, dedication, and sacrifice—the very basic requirements of true discipleship—but in my experience, the communities that begin to embrace true inclusion in these sorts of tangible, quantifiable ways all become powerful forces of healing and justice in their communities and beyond.

If you have any other suggestions for ways communities can embrace true inclusion or would like to share your communities experience with it, please send me an email anytime at trueinclusionbook@gmail.com.

Appendix 2

Resources for Further Study

Anderson, David A. *Multicultural Ministry: Finding Your Church's Unique Rhythm.* Zondervan, 2004.

Burrus, Virginia, and Catherine Keller. *Toward a Theology of Eros: Transfiguring Passion at the Limits of Discipline.* Fordham University Press, 2006.

Edman, Elizabeth M. *Queer Virtue: What LGBTQ People Know About Life and Love and How It Can Revitalize Christianity.* Beacon Press, 2016.

Flunder, Yvette A. *Where the Edge Gathers: Building a Community of Radical Inclusion.* The Pilgrim Press, 2005.

Gunning Francis, Leah. *Ferguson and Faith: Sparking Leadership and Awakening Community.* Chalice Press, 2015.

Gushee, David P., et al. *Changing Our Mind: A Call from America's Leading Evangelical Ethics Scholar for Full Acceptance of LGBT Christians in the Church.* Read the Spirit Books, an Imprint of David Crumm Media, LLC, 2015.

Hartke, Austen. *Transforming: The Bible and the Lives of Transgender Christians.* Westminster John Knox Press, 2018.

Kirk, J. R. Daniel. *Jesus Have I Loved, but Paul?: A Narrative Approach to the Problem of Pauline Christianity.* Baker Academic, 2011.

Lee, Deborah Jian. *Rescuing Jesus: How People of Color, Women, and Queer Christians Are Reclaiming Evangelicalism.* Beacon, 2016.

Martin, Dale B. *Sex and the Single Savior: Gender and Sexuality in Biblical Interpretation.* Westminster John Knox Press, 2006.

Murchu, Diarmuid O. *Inclusivity: A Gospel Mandate.* Claretian Publications, 2016.

Oliveto, Karen P. *Our Strangely Warmed Hearts: Coming Out into God's Call*. Abingdon Press, 2018.

Pearson, Carlton. *The Gospel of Inclusion: Reaching beyond Religious Fundamentalism to the True Love of God and Self*. Atria Books, 2008.

Reynolds, Thomas E. *Vulnerable Communion: A Theology of Disability and Hospitality*. Brazos Press, 2008.

Robertson, Brandan, editor. *Our Witness: The Unheard Stories of LGBT+ Christians*. Cascade Books, 2018.

Sanders, Cody J. *Microaggressions in Ministry: Confronting the Hidden Violence of Everyday Church*. Westminster John Knox Press, 2015.

Smith, Mitzi Jane. *Womanist Sass and Talk Back: Social (In)Justice, Intersectionality, and Biblical Interpretation*. Cascade Books, 2018.

Snider, Phil, editor. *Justice Calls: Sermons of Welcome and Affirmation*. Cascade Books, 2016.

Spina, Frank Anthony. *The Faith of the Outsider: Exclusion and Inclusion in the Biblical Story*. Eerdmans, 2005.

Thurman, Howard. *Jesus and the Disinherited*. Beacon Press, 1996.

Volf, Miroslav. *Exclusion and Embrace: A Theological Exploration of Identity, Otherness, and Reconciliation*. Abingdon Press, 2008.

Webb, William J. *Corporal Punishment in the Bible: A Redemptive-Movement Hermeneutic for Troubling Texts*. IVP Academic, 2011.

Webb, William J. *Slaves, Women & Homosexuals: Exploring the Hermeneutics of Cultural Analysis*. InterVarsity Press , 2001.

Wilder, Courtney. *Disability, Faith, and the Church: Inclusion and Accommodation in Contemporary Congregations*. Praeger, 2016.

Wytsma, Ken. *The Myth of Equality: Uncovering the Roots of Injustice and Privilege*. IVP Books, 2017.

Zerai, Assata. *Intersectionality in Intentional Communities: The Struggle for Inclusivity in Multicultural U.S. Protestant Congregations*. Lexington Books, 2016.